LATINA Mythica

by
Bonnie A. Catto

Illustrations by
Christopher J. White

Bolchazy-Carducci Publishers, Inc.
Wauconda, Illinois USA

Editor
Laurie Haight Keenan

Contributing Editor
Andrew J. Adams

Design and Typography
Adam Velez

Cover Illustration
"The Escape: Icarus and the Minotaur" © 2006 Thom Kapheim

Illustrations
© 2006 Christopher J. White

Cartography by
The Ohio University Cartographic Center

Latina Mythica
by Bonnie A. Catto

© copyright 2006 Bolchazy-Carducci Publishers, Inc.
All rights reserved.

Bolchazy-Carducci Publishers, Inc.
1000 Brown Street, Unit 101
Wauconda, Illinois 60084 USA
www.bolchazy.com

Printed in the United States of America
2006
by United Graphics

ISBN-13: 978-0-86516-599-1
ISBN-10: 0-86516-599-8

Library of Congress Cataloging-in-Publication Data

Catto, Bonnie A., 1951-
 Latina mythica / by Bonnie A. Catto ; illustrations by Christopher J. White.
   p. cm.
 Includes bibliographical references.
 ISBN-13: 978-0-86516-599-1 (pbk. : alk. paper)
 ISBN-10: 0-86516-599-8 (pbk. : alk. paper)
  1. Latin language--Readers--Mythology. 2. Mythology, Classical--Problems, exercises, etc. 3. Latin language--Grammar--Problems, exercises, etc. I. Title.

PA2095.C3365 2005
478.6'421--dc22

2005032576

Contents

Acknowledgments v
Preface vii
Map of Places Mentioned in the Myths xiii

1. The Olympian Gods 1
2. Creation: The First Gods and the Titans 11
3. The Battle of the Gods 17
4. Prometheus: Inventor and Benefactor; Pandora 25
5. Prometheus Punished 31
6. The Ages of Man 39
7. The Flood: Deucalion and Pyrrha 47
8. Theseus and the Minotaur; Ariadne 55
9. The Fates of Ariadne and Aegeus 63
10. Daedalus and Icarus: Man-Powered Flight 69
11. The History of Bacchus: Semele and Pentheus 77
12. Oedipus: Riddle and Discovery 85
13. Oedipus' Further Destiny: Seven Against Thebes, Antigone 97
14. The Birth of Hercules 105
15. The Labors of Hercules 111
16. Jason's Quest for the Golden Fleece 123
17. Medea's Vengeance 131

18.	Leda and the Swan: The Birth of Helen, Clytaemnestra and the Dioscuri	145
19.	The Prelude to War I: The Wedding of Peleus and Thetis; The Judgment of Paris	151
20.	The Prelude to War II: The Abduction of Helen; The Sacrifice of Iphigenia	157
	Genealogical Charts	171
	Ancient Sources Cited	177
	Bibliography	181
	Vocabulary	185

Illustrations by Christopher J. White

Mercury—Winged Feet	9
Saturn and Ops (Rhea)	23
Prometheus' Liver Eaten by the Eagle	37
Theseus and the Minotaur	61
Daedalus Watches Icarus' Fall	75
Juno's Vengeance against Semele	83
Oedipus Blinded	95
Hercules Strangles the Nemean Lion	121
Medea Kills Her Children	143
Agamemnon Sacrifices His Daughter, Iphigenia	169

Acknowledgments

Any book is a collaborative effort. There are many people whom I would like to thank for their contributions to this text. Despite the kind assistance of many people I am sure that the book is not perfect. Any errors that remain are, of course, solely my own.

The idea for this book arose from my experiences in teaching elementary and intermediate Latin courses at Assumption College. For the mid-term and final exams I often created simplified Latin versions of some of the great myths of antiquity. The students seemed to enjoy these versions and to benefit from them. Therefore I would like to thank my students who acted as both my inspiration and test subjects. In the Fall of 2003, I used a preliminary version of the first half of the book with my students in Latin 201, and I am grateful for their positive reaction and helpful assistance. It is much easier to see flaws and places that need expansion in the presence of students than in the isolation of one's study.

I would also like to thank Assumption College for its support of this book. I began its composition during a sabbatical year in 2002–03. The Information Technology Services at Assumption, in particular Mark Brooks, Joe LePain, Carmella Murphy, and Tom St. John helped me cope with the transition to a new computer configuration and with the printing of macrons. Our Foreign Language Department Secretary, Cathy Fuller, was also consistently helpful by maintaining a genuine interest in the book's progress, by knowing the right people to contact in various offices, and by doing it all with a smile. My colleague in Classics, Professor Anne B. Nelson, has been most generous with her support and advice. Professor Anne Leinster Windham in Art assisted me by locating art resources.

I would also like to thank Bolchazy-Carducci Publishers, Inc. for their encouragement and support of the project. Dr. Ladislaus Bolchazy sent me the transcripts of his series of radio programs on comparative mythology. These were very helpful in figuring out what myths to include and what approaches to take. I am particularly grateful to Editor Laurie Haight Keenan for her keen attention to detail and nuance. During the writing of the book she advised me on numerous matters and kept me going by gentle queries about my progress. Towards the end she showed admirable patience in enduring a constant flurry of e-mails regarding wayward illustrations and other matters. Editor LeaAnn Osburn helped with the technical aspects of printing macrons and with her friendly interest. I would particularly like to thank the two anonymous readers of the original manuscript. Their many detailed and perceptive suggestions and meticulous corrections have greatly improved the final version.

Professor Emeritus Gilbert Lawall of the University of Massachusetts, Amherst has offered encouragement and support. He provided the Latipal font that I used to create the macrons.

I appreciate the fine collection of classical materials at the Mount Holyoke College Library, which is near my home. It was most useful for consulting reference materials and classical texts. Indeed I also remember working there many years ago with Jane Reid, author of *The Oxford Guide to Mythology in the Arts*, a book which I used extensively for the "Cultural Influences" sections of each chapter.

My friends Bruce Plichta, Bill "Seve" Shaheen, and Marv Weaver willingly listened to my ramblings and inquired about the book's progress as we ambled around the golf course. Roberta Adams, Professor of English at Fitchburg State College, also heard my mutterings and provided an always sympathetic ear.

I would also like to thank members of my family. In particular, I am most grateful to my nephew Christopher J. White, an art student at Virginia Commonwealth University, who has created original art works for some of the chapters. It was a pleasure to work with Chris on this challenging assignment that required him to familiarize himself with totally new material and to use his creative vision. My sister, Heather White, Chris' mother, also helped me clarify my thinking as we talked through some of the difficulties in composition in the last chapters. My sister Maddie Sifantus understood my interest in mythology and was good company at various productions of classical plays. As always, I thank my parents, Lina and Harold MacNeill, who have unfailingly offered their love and support over the years. I am indeed lucky to have such wonderful parents who are still alive and well in their 90s. Finally, I thank my husband Alistair who helped me put things in perspective, proferred cups of tea in the a.m., and in many ways kept me going so that this book could finally be completed.

Preface

Purpose

Many students begin the study of Latin because of an interest in mythology, yet most Latin textbooks include very few references even to major Greco-Roman myths. Familiarity with these myths is a basic element of cultural literacy and enables students to appreciate the myriad works of art, literature, and music that reveal classical influences. Many Latin textbooks also do not provide continuous narrative passages, which help students better understand Latin sentence construction and the flow of one idea into another. This text aims to remedy both deficiencies by providing a collection of major myths written in Latin of gradually increasing difficulty. The stories may be used as in-class sight reading, as assigned work, or as reading passages for tests. In writing the simplified versions I have attempted, as much as possible, to use the vocabulary and phraseology of the Latin source for the myth, whether Plautus, Catullus, Horace, Lucretius, Vergil, Horace, Seneca, or others. For some myths or sections of myths there is no definitive Latin source; in these cases I have nonetheless tried to create Latin in the style of the first and second centuries BC and AD. Thus, though the stories are not technically "real" Latin, they are modeled upon the authentic texts. As the chapters proceed the Latin becomes closer to the original sources, since students will have a greater vocabulary and be better able to understand more complex sentence structure. Each myth is preceded by an introduction that gives necessary background information and refers to the source of the myth in Latin as well as in Greek. Students may enjoy reading the full version of a myth in English translation or researching the development of a myth and its variants over time.

Selections

There is such a marvellous wealth of Greco-Roman myths that it would be impossible to include all the myths. In the process of selection I have tried, first, to feature the major myths that have had the greatest cultural influence. Myths are not necessarily pretty stories; some, particularly the early myths of divine succession, are quite graphic in their violence. I have not avoided these myths but have tried to temper the description of the violence.

Some of the myths have been included in other Latin readers or texts that are readily available (e.g., Groton and May, *38 Latin Stories to Accompany Wheelock's Latin*; Goldman and Nyenhuis, *Latin via Ovid*; two booklets from the American

Classical League: Morse, *Fabulae Latinae* and Brothers and Neurohr, *Ten Classical Myths*; the older text by Ritchie, *Fabulae Faciles*). I have tried not to replicate what has already been done well by others. For instance, I have not written a separate account of the myth of Pandora's box (Groton and May, Chapter 1). Rather, I have included the story of Pandora in the larger context of the myth of Prometheus and Epimetheus. Similarly, as part of the prelude to the Trojan War, after an account of the Marriage of Peleus and Thetis I have included a full treatment of the Judgment of Paris in Chapter 19, although Groton and May devoted their Chapter 19 to the same theme.

Since this is a Latin textbook, I have primarily used Roman names for the gods and heroes. Since students do need to be familiar with their Greek names, these are included for reference. In Chapter One there is a comparative chart of the Greek and Roman names for easy reference.

In organizing the myths I have presented them roughly by mythological chronology and by mythological cycle (e.g., Prometheus and related stories, Theseus and Cretan legend, Oedipus, etc.). Thus, after the first chapter introducing the main Roman gods with their Greek equivalents, I have included various creation stories followed by the rise of Jupiter to power, the birth of mankind and the role of Prometheus, and Deucalion and Pyrrha. There follow stories of mythical figures prior to the Trojan War, such as Theseus, Oedipus and the Theban cycle, Hercules, and Jason and Medea. The final chapters set the scene for the Trojan War.

A planned second volume will describe the Trojan War and its aftermath, with stories drawn from the *Iliad* and the *Odyssey*. The second volume will also include myths about underworld visits, the metamorphic loves of Jupiter, and some particularly Roman myths, such as Aeneas' escape from Troy, Camilla, the death of Turnus, and Romulus and Remus.

In writing the stories I pondered how best to represent the complexity of myths that include many variants without either oversimplification or unnecessary confusion for the reader. My solution has been to provide within the readings some of the variants as alternative questions (e.g., did Helen go willingly with Paris or was she abducted?). Thus the students can reach their own conclusions, as in a book with multiple endings.

METHODOLOGY

This book is designed for students who have already been introduced to the basics of Latin grammar (at a minimum one semester of college-level Latin or one year of high school Latin). More advanced students may also enjoy the readings, since by relatively rapid reading and comprehension they gain a sense of mastery over the language. The book can readily be used by students of any standard Latin text, since all vocabulary is provided either on the page facing the text or in the End

Vocabulary. I have used the book as a way to refresh and reinforce students' grammar and vocabulary while providing interesting and important content. Since the readings gradually increase in grammatical complexity, this book can be used as a grammatical review in a narrative context. The grammar assumed in the book is based upon the first twenty-two chapters of *Wheelock's Latin* as revised by Richard A. LaFleur (HarperCollins Publishers, © 2000), a standard college-level textbook. Thus this book assumes knowledge of the following:

Grammatical Forms:

Nouns: all forms of the five declensions

Adjectives: all simple forms plus numerals. Comparatives and superlatives, when used, have been given as vocabulary. Similarly participles have been treated as adjectives and given as vocabulary.

Pronouns: demonstrative, intensive, interrogative, personal, and reflexive pronouns.

Verbs: all indicative forms of the four conjugations in the active and passive voices. The present active and present passive infinitives. Present imperatives. Conjugation of *sum* and *possum* in the indicative mood.

Syntax: the normal use of the cases including prepositional phrases; genitive of the whole; ablatives of agent, means, accompaniment, manner, time, place from which, and separation. Agreement of adjectives with nouns. Agreement of subject with verb. Complementary infinitive.

Teachers will note that the book does not assume knowledge of deponent verbs, indirect discourse, the subjunctive mood and its related constructions, the ablative absolute, passive periphrastic, conditions other than simple conditions, and more advanced grammar. Some of these constructions do indeed occur in the readings, but each time the construction is explained in the accompanying notes.

In providing vocabulary for the readings, I tried to avoid an excessive and intimidating listing. Therefore I also decided to assume knowledge of the vocabulary included in the first twenty-two chapters of the Wheelock text; these words are not given in the facing vocabulary unless they are used in an unusual way. Since there is considerable agreement among major Latin texts on the order of introduction both of grammar and vocabulary, vocabulary should not be a great problem for those using other texts. Once a word has been defined as new vocabulary in a particular chapter, it is not given again in that chapter. Although each chapter is arranged in mythological sequence, I realize that there may not be time for students to read all the selections. Thus I have repeated unknown vocabulary from one chapter to the next so that the chapters can be read individually. Once a word has already appeared in two chapters, however, it is generally not given again. Of course, all words that appear more than once are included in the end Vocabulary where students may consult words unfamiliar to them. It is assumed that students can easily recognize first and second declension proper names so that these are not always included in the facing vocabulary. Third declension proper names are glossed in the vocabulary. My English definitions are based partly upon *Wheelock*, if the word appears in that text, and more often on *The Oxford Latin Dictionary*. Also, as the chapters proceed, less vocabulary is given. It is increasingly assumed that students can infer the meaning of compound words from their components (e.g., *deduco, devenio*). Words that have direct English derivatives (e.g., *excito, horribile, omen, senior, terribile*) are not given unless students need information about their inflection. Of course, all words are included in the end Vocabulary where students may consult the Latin forms. In general, in the matter of vocabulary I believe that if I have erred, I have done so by inclusion rather than exclusion.

The readings are mostly designed to be read in one class or assignment. There are exceptions, like the first chapter, which introduces the major Olympian gods. This chapter could be divided into separate readings for the fourteen gods that are included. Similarly, the readings on Oedipus and the final two chapters, which include interrelated myths, could be divided among class sessions.

Although the readings are based primarily on poetic sources, this is a prose text. Therefore I have somewhat simplified poetic word order and have not replicated devices such as synchysis and chiasmus. As the text proceeds, the word order becomes more varied and closer to the original sources. In many instances, to avoid endless vocabulary lists, I have substituted a more prosaic word with which the student may be familiar for a more obscure poetic one. I have tried to create realistic Latin using proper cases and constructions. This has been problematic because of the limited grammatical knowledge of students who have studied only basic grammar. As noted above, I have restricted myself from using the ablative absolute, indirect statement, deponent verbs, most participles, and subjunctive constructions. On occasion I could not avoid these constructions; in those instances I have given a full explanation and often a translation in the notes. I have made frequent use of *necesse est* with the accusative and infinitive, but again I have explained the construction the first few times it appears. Also, I have used *esse* in indirect statement when it can be simply translated *to be* without knowledge of the larger construction. I have used perfect passive participles fairly often, but I have treated them simply as adjectives in the vocabulary. Even adverbs posed a problem since the forms are not introduced until Chapter 32 of *Wheelock*. Thus the vocabulary may seem to include an unnecessarily large number of adverbs for students of other texts who have already studied them.

The text includes macrons (long marks) which I believe are helpful in differentiating words and forms as well as in preparing to read poetry. For the placement of macrons, I have relied upon *Chambers-Murray Latin-English Dictionary*, by Sir William Smith and Sir John Lockwood (Edinburgh: 1976). This dictionary is more complete than either the *Oxford Latin Dictionary* or Lewis and Short's *Latin Dictionary* in its inclusion of macrons. For instance, in the Chambers-Murray dictionary entries there are macrons on *īnfāns, coniūnx, crēscō, and iūssī*. These are absent in Oxford and Lewis and Short.

Each chapter includes a number of features. In addition to the list of ancient sources for the myth, students will find under the heading "Cultural Influences" references to some of the literary, artistic, musical, cinematic, and even cartoon works that have been influenced by the myth. Indeed, the whimsical cover illustration of Icarus and the Minotaur by Thom Kapheim provides one such example of an updated, contemporary interpretation of myth. Of course, an exhaustive list of such works would obviously be impossible. Therefore I have tried to include references from various periods and media. I have focused upon post-classical material, since references on Greek vases, for instance, can be fairly easily found in various texts and internet sites. Of particular value is *The Oxford Guide to Mythology in the Arts*, which students can consult for further examples and for details of the location and other particulars of most of the included references. For further material students and teachers may also consult the internet resources listed in the bibliography. Teachers may want to use the references I have included to create projects for students in tracing the influence of a particular myth.

Each chapter also includes a number of Grammar and Comprehension Questions that aim to assist students both in translating the material and developing a full understanding of the myth. Sometimes the grammar questions hint that students should look beyond the obvious in identifying a form. For instance, just because a noun occurs first in a clause does not mean it is the subject: one must look also at the verb!

When a grammatical question asks students to identify a **form**, this can be answered as follows:

> **For nouns and adjectives:** What declension is the noun? What case, number, and gender?
>
> **For pronouns:** the above questions. Also identify the type of pronoun.
>
> **For verbs:** What conjugation is the verb? What person, number, tense, and voice?

When a grammatical question asks students the **function** of a word, this can be answered as follows:

For nouns and pronouns: Is it the subject, genitive of possession, indirect object, direct object, object of a preposition, or one of the various ablative constructions?

For adjectives and pronouns: What noun does the adjective modify following the rules regarding agreement by gender, number, and case? If the word is a relative pronoun, what is its antecedent, with which it agrees in gender and number?

For verbs: Is it the main verb, the verb in a relative clause, a complementary infinitive, etc.?

Each chapter also includes Discussion Questions that are intended to stir the imagination of students as well as to show the relevance of the materal in their contemporary world. Sometimes I have also suggested projects that might inspire student interest.

The book ends with a brief bibliography of basic mythological reference books and some internet resources. Again, no such tool can be exhaustive in a text of this length, but the references included should enable students and teachers to find more detailed information on the myths and their influence.

The world of myth is still very much a part of our culture in the twenty-first century. I hope that students and teachers alike will enjoy these timeless stories.

BONNIE A. CATTO
Assumption College

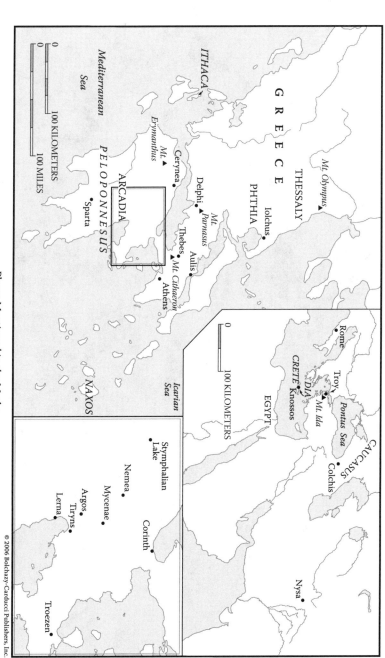

Places Mentioned in the Myths

Chapter One

THE OLYMPIAN GODS

The Romans, like the Greeks, believed in and worshipped a multiplicity of gods, both male and female. The famous temple in Rome, the Pantheon (meaning "all gods"), was built in 27–25 BC, but there were also individual temples for all the gods and goddesses. Originally these gods represented the various powers of nature. As literature and art developed, many of the gods also developed distinctive personalities. Just like humans, the gods didn't always get along with one another; their conflicts and their relationships with humans are the source of some of the most interesting mythological stories. In art, in particular, the gods are often easily recognized by objects that they carry, their clothing, or even their association with certain animals.

There are generations of gods. Gods are born but of course cannot die. Jupiter and his fellow Olympians are the third generation of gods to come to power. Many of the Olympian gods have children, both with other gods and with humans. Some of these children are themselves divine, while others are human. In addition to the major gods and goddesses, there are many lesser gods who affect humans, some of whom you will read about in this book. The following selection describes the major Olympian gods, their powers, and their attributes.

multōs deōs esse et multās deās: accusative nouns in indirect statement (see Wheelock, Ch. 25). Translate *esse* "existed."
habitō (1) - *to live, dwell*
cuique: dative of possession (see p. 443, Wheelock) *for each*
prōvincia, -ae, f. - *special function, command*
Iuppiter, Iovis, Iovī, Iovem, Iove, m. - *Jupiter*
fulmen, -minis, n. - *thunderbolt*
portō (1) - *to carry*
gubernō (1) - *to control*
aquila, -ae, f. - *eagle*

Iūnō, -ōnis, f. - *Juno*
mātrimōnium, -iī, n. - *marriage*
pāvō, -vōnis, m. - *peacock*
adsum, -esse, -fuī, -futūrus - *to be present*

pontus, -ī, m. - *sea*
tridēns, -entis, m. - *trident, three-pronged spear*
Plūtō, -tōnis, m. - *Pluto*
mortuus, -ī, m. - *dead person, corpse*
focus, -ī, m. - *hearth*
Vestālis, -is, f. - *Vestal virgin*
aeternus, -a, -um - *eternal*
flamma, -ae, f. - *flame*
Mars, Martis, m. - *Mars*
conditor, -tōris, m. - *founder*
Venus, -neris, f. - *Venus*
pulchritūdō, -dinis, f. - *beauty*
incertus, -a, -um - *uncertain, in doubt*

Volcānus, -ī, m. - *Vulcan, god of fire*
officīna, -ae, f. - *workshop, place where something is made, forge*
incendium, -iī, n. - *fire*
validus, -a, -um - *strong*
claudus, -a, -um - *lame*

Grammar and Comprehension Questions

1) What case is *fulmen* and what is its function?
2) What case is *mortuōrum* and what is its function?
3) What is the relationship between Jupiter, Neptune, and Pluto?
4) What emotion do humans feel towards Pluto? Why?
5) What is the case and function of *Martem*?
6) What case is *incendiō* and what is its function?

The Olympian Gods   3

Rōmānī cōgitābant multōs deōs esse et multās deās. Deī et deae habitābant in monte Olympō. Cuique deō erat prōvincia sua.

Iuppiter est rēx deōrum. Iuppiter etiam est deus caelī et **fulmen** portat. Iuppiter tempestātem gubernat. Saepe vidēs aquilam cum Iove.

Iūnō, uxor Iovis, est dea mātrimōniī. Saepe cum Iūnōne pāvō adest.

Neptūnus, frāter Iovis, pontum gubernat et tridentem portat.

Plūtō, etiam frāter Iovis, terram **mortuōrum** gubernat; omnēs vīrī et fēminae hunc deum timent.

Vesta, soror Iovis, focum servat. Septem Vestālēs aeternam flammam Rōmae servant.

Mars, fīlius Iovis et Iūnōnis, est deus bellī. Fīlius Martis est Rōmulus, conditor Rōmae.

Venus est dea amōris et pulchritūdinis. Pater Veneris est incertus, sed saepe Venus vocat Iovem patrem. Venus est uxor Volcānī sed **Martem** amat. Venus est māter Aenēae, patris Rōmānōrum.

Volcānus, fīlius Iovis et Iūnōnis, est deus officīnae et **incendiō** labōrat. Volcānus est validus sed claudus.

Discussion Questions

1) What role does the eagle play? How do mortals perceive it?
2) What is the other relationship between Jupiter and Juno?
3) Examine versions of the birth/origin of Venus in mythology by consulting a text or website.

artificium, -iī, n. - *handicraft, craftsmanship*

Athēnae, -ārum, f. pl. - *the city of Athens*

templum, -ī, n. - *temple*

Parthenon: *the Parthenon,* meaning *the maiden*

galea, -ae, f. - *helmet*

gestō (1) - *to wear*

hasta, -ae, f. - *spear*

Lātōna, -ae, f. - *Latona,* in Greek Leto, daughter of the Titan gods Phoebe and Coeus

geminus, -ī, m. - *twin*

Apollō, -linis, m. - *Apollo*

laureātus, -a, -um - *wearing a laurel wreath*

lyra, -ae, f. - *lyre,* a stringed musical instrument

poētica, -ae, f. - *poetry*

vātēs, -is, m. - *prophet*

cōtīdiē (adv.) - *daily*

currus, -ūs, m. - *chariot*

agitō (1) - *to drive, ride*

Phoebus, -ī, m. - *Phoebus;* in Greek means *shining, brilliant*

vēnātrīx, -trīcis, f. - *huntress*

arcus, -ūs, m. - *bow*

silva, -ae, f. - *forest*

lūna, -ae, f. - *moon*

Maia, -ae, f. - *Maia,* daughter of the Titan Atlas

nuntius, -iī, m. - *messenger*

cādūceus, -ī, m. - *caduceus, magic wand.* The caduceus is now used as the symbol for medicine.

ālātus, -a, -um - *winged*

pilleus, -ī, m. - *cap*

solea, -ae, f. - *sandal*

celeritās, -tātis, f. - *speed, swiftness*

fūr, fūris, m. - *thief*

fraudātor, -tōris, m. - *trickster*

īnfāns, -antis - *infant*

taurus, -ī, m. - *bull*

surripiō, -ere, -ripuī, -reptum - *to take away secretly, steal*

Grammar and Comprehension Questions

1) What is unusual about the parentage of Minerva?
2) What tense is *creāvit*?
3) What case and number are *multa officia*? What is their grammatical function?
4) How many functions does Apollo have?
5) What characteristic do Minerva and Diana share?
6) What tense is *vocābant*?

The Olympian Gods — 5

Minerva, fīlia Iovis, est sine mātre. Minerva est dea artificiī. Minerva virōs nōn amat, quod virgō est. In Graeciā nōmen Minervae est Athēna. Graecī vocant clārum templum Minervae in urbe Athēnīs "Parthenon." Minerva galeam saepe gestat et hastam tenet.

Cum deā Lātōnā Iuppiter **creāvit** geminōs, puerum et puellam. Puer est Apollo; puella est Diāna.

Apollō est bellus deus et **multa officia** habet. Saepe laureātus lyram portat. Apollō est deus mūsicae, poēticae, et medicīnae. Apollō etiam est vātēs. Cōtīdiē in caelō vidēs Apollinem, quod Apollō currum sōlis agitat. Saepe Rōmānī **vocābant** Apollinem Phoebum.

Diāna, soror Apollinis, est virgō et vēnātrīx. Saepe arcum portat. Diāna silvās et animālia cūrat. Rōmānī etiam vocābant Diānam "Lūnam" quod Diāna est dea lūnae.

Mercurius est fīlius Iovis et deae Maiae. Mercurius est nuntius deōrum. Cādūceum portat. Ālātus pilleus et ālātae soleae celeritātem Mercuriī dēmōnstrant. Deus est etiam fūr et fraudātor. Īnfāns Mercurius taurōs Apollinis surripuit!

Discussion Questions

1) What English word can you find that comes from *gubernō?*
2) In what context(s) was the name Mercury used in the twentieth century and why?
3) What does the caduceus look like? Where else might you see it?

Caduceus

iuvenis, -is, m./f. - *youth*
Semelē, -lēs, f. - *Semele,* princess of Thebes
prīmō (adv.) - *at first, first*
putō (1) - *to think, consider*
esse: in indirect statement (see Wheelock, Ch. 25), translate *was*
mox (adv.) - *soon*
vīnum, -ī, n. - *wine*
adōrō (1) - *to worship*
corōnātus, -a, -um - *crowned, wreathed*
hedera, -ae, f. - *ivy*
pōculum, -ī, n. - *drinking-vessel, cup, bowl*
40 **Bacchantēs, -um, f. pl.** - *Bacchantes,* women devoted to the worship of the god Bacchus
satyrus, -ī, m. - *satyr,* a demi-god of wild places; half-man, half-goat

comitō (1) - *to accompany, attend*
Cerēs, Cereris, f. - *Ceres,* the goddess of grain
cultūra, -ae, f. - *agriculture*
fēriae, -ārum, f. pl. - *religious festival, holy day, holiday*
agō, -ere, ēgī, actum - here, *to hold*
nōtus, -a, -um - *famous*
fābula, -ae, f. - *story, tale*
absēns, -entis - *absent, missing*
lūgeō, -ēre, lūxī, lūctum - *to mourn, lament*
45 **hiems, -mis, f.** - *winter*
sex (indeclinable adj.) - *six*
mēnsis, -is, m. - *month*
gaudeō, -ēre, gāvīsus sum - *to be glad, rejoice*
aestās, -tātis, f. - *summer*
referēbat: *brought back*

Grammar and Comprehension Questions

1) How can you recognize Bacchus?
2) What person and number is *potes*?
3) What case is *hederā*? What is its function?
4) What caused Ceres to abandon her duties?

Bacchus est iuvenis. Deus est fīlius Iovis et mortālis Semelēs.
Prīmō Graecī nōn putābant Bacchum esse deum. Mox Graecī
Bacchum, deum vīnī, laudābant et adōrābant. **Potes** vidēre Bacchum
corōnātum **hederā**. Saepe Bacchus pōculum portat. Multae fēminae,
Bacchantēs, et multī satyrī deum comitant.

Cerēs est Māter Terra, dea agrī cultūrae. Dea est soror Iovis,
Iūnōnis, Neptūnī, et Plūtōnis. Graecī magnās fēriās deae agēbant.
Potes legere nōtam fābulam dē Prōserpīnā, fīliā Cereris. Plūtō
Prōserpīnam rapuit. Cerēs absentem fīliam lūgēbat et agrī cultūram
nōn cūrābat. Hiems igitur erat. Post sex mēnsēs Plūtō Prōserpīnam
līberāvit. Tum Cerēs gaudēbat et aestātem referēbat.

Discussion Questions

1) On what sort of vessel would you expect to find pictures of Bacchus?
2) What name for an agricultural product derives from Ceres?
3) What is the mythical explanation for winter?

Jupiter with his eagle

Cultural Influences

Art: Sandro Botticelli, *Venus and Mars* (1480–90); Paolo Veronese, *Mars and Venus United by Love* (1578–80); Nicolas Poussin, *Mars and Venus* (c. 1630), and numerous other examples.

Music: Gustav Holst, *The Planets* (1914–16), orchestral suite: 1) Mars, the Bringer of War, 2) Venus, the Bringer of Peace, 3) Mercury, the Winged Messenger, 4) Jupiter, the Bringer of Jollity, 5) Saturn, the Bringer of Old Age, 6) Uranus, the Magician, 7) Neptune, the Mystic. Saturn and Uranus are gods from the previous generation about whom you will learn in Chapter 2. In popular music Frankie Avalon's "Venus," Connie Frances' "Stupid Cupid" with lyrics by Neil Sedaka and Howie Greenfield, and Jimmy Clanton's "Venus in Blue Jeans."

Mythical Variations

Traditionally the Roman gods have been identified with their Greek counterparts who have similar functions. A list of the equivalent Greek and Roman names is found below. You should familiarize yourself with the Greek names as well. You will note that some gods have multiple names that represent their various functions or cult sites.

Roman	**Greek**
Jupiter, Jove	Zeus
Iuno	Hera
Neptune	Poseidon
Pluto, Dis, Orcus, Hades	Hades
Vesta	Hestia
Mars	Ares
Vulcan	Hephaistus
Venus	Aphrodite
Minerva	Athena, Pallas
Apollo, Phoebus	Apollo, Phoebus
Diana	Artemis
Mercury	Hermes
Bacchus, Liber	Dionysus, Bacchus
Ceres	Demeter

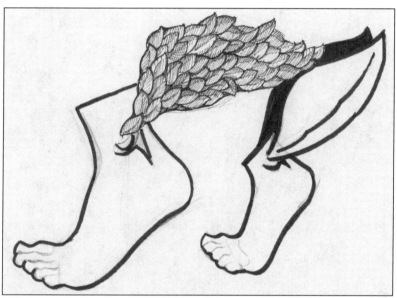

Mercury—Winged Feet

© 2006 Christopher J. White

Chapter Two

CREATION: THE FIRST GODS AND THE TITANS

All peoples throughout history have tried to explain the creation or genesis of the world. The Greeks and Romans provided a number of explanations. The earliest complete mythological explanation is found in *Theogony* 105ff. (Birth of the Gods), an epic poem by the Greek poet Hesiod (c. 700 BC). The original state of chaos (in Greek, a gaping void or chasm) ended with the spontaneous appearance of earth (Gaia), Tartarus (the underworld), and Eros (love). Eros was necessary to explain the creative impulse by which these original gods, especially Gaia, produced all the others. Gaia produced sky (Uranus) and then together with him gave birth to the second generation of the gods, the Titans. The Roman poet Ovid in the first century BC begins his epic *Metamorphoses* with the ultimate metamorphosis: the creation of the universe, order from chaos. In his version Ovid simultaneously provides two conflicting views: 1) the order in the universe was divinely created, or 2) order spontaneously arose from chaos. This latter view is similar to the views of the Roman epic poet Lucretius, who discusses the materialistic view of creation in Book 5. 64ff. of *De rerum natura* (On the Nature of Things). The following reading passage is modeled first on Ovid and then on the earlier Hesiodic version of the birth of the second generation of gods, the Titans.

SOURCES

Homer in *Iliad* 14.201ff. provides a brief description of the early gods, in which Oceanus and Tethys (in Hesiod, children of Gaia and Uranos) are called the original gods. The comic poet Aristophanes in his play *Birds* 683ff. (414 BC) gives a version similar to Hesiod's, in which, naturally, birds play a prominent role. Chaos had two children, Erebus (Darkness) and "black-winged" Night. Night produced an egg, from which hatched Eros, a deity with golden wings. Apollodorus, the Greek mythographer (probably second century AD) in *Bibliotheca* (The Library) provides a summary of earlier views, which are fundamentally consistent with the Hesiodic version.

Students will probably also be familiar with the version of creation from *Genesis* in the Old Testament of the Bible. In the biblical version "God created the heaven and the earth. And the earth was without form, and void." As in the Greco-Roman version, God also used a process of separation. He created light and separated it from the darkness. He created earth and separated it from water.

vultus, -ūs, m. - *appearance, look, aspect*
elementum, -ī, n. - *element*
sōl, sōlis, m. - *sun*
fulgeō, -ēre, fūlsī - *to shine, gleam*
pendeō, -ēre, pependī - *to hang suspended, hang*

pontus, -ī, m. - *sea*
circumdō (1) - *to surround*
āēr, āeris, m. - *air*
mixtus, -a, -um - *mixed*
sēparō (1) - *to separate, divide*

5

Grammar and Comprehension Questions

1) What did the Greeks call the initial state of the universe?
2) What began the process of the creation of the universe as we know it?
3) What tense are *fulgēbat* and *pendēbat*?
4) What verb governs *terrās*?

Ante pontum et terram et caelum ūnus vultus erat in tōtō mundō. Graecī hunc vultum "chaos" vocābant. Multa elementa erant in magnō bellō. Nihil erat in locō suō. Nūllus sōl **fulgēbat**, nūlla terra in caelō **pendēbat**. Nūllus pontus terram circumdabat. Terra, pontus, et āēr erant, sed omnia elementa erant mixta. Tum deus, aut nātūra, **terrās** ā caelō, pontum ā terrā sēparāvit. 5

Discussion Questions

1) Compare closely the Greco-Roman and Biblical versions of creation.
2) What does the word chaos mean today? Has the meaning changed?

Gāia, -ae, f. - *Gaia*, original goddess, mother earth
Ūranus, -ī, m. - *Uranus*, sky god, son and spouse of Gaia
mātrimōnium, -iī, n. - *marriage*
plūrimus, -a, -um - *very many*
generō (1) - *to produce, give birth to*
duodecim (indeclinable adj.) - *twelve*
Tītānus, -ī, m. - *Titan*, child of Gaia and Uranus
sex (indeclinable adj.) - *six*
Cronus, -ī, m. - *Cronus*, the Roman Saturn
minimus, -a, -um - *youngest*
10 mōnstrum, -ī, n. - *monster*
Cyclops, -lōpis, m. - *Cyclops*
Gigās, -gantis, m. - *Giant*
validus, -a, -um - *strong*
fulmen, -minis, n. - *thunderbolt*

gubernō (1) - *to control, govern*
frōns, -ntis, f. - *forehead*
brācchium, -iī, n. - *arm*
quīnquāgintā (indeclinable adj.) - *fifty*
15 retrūdō, -ere - *to push back*
labōrō (1) - here, *to suffer* (in childbirth)
suscēnseō, -ēre, -uī - *to be angry*
Sāturnus, -ī, m. - *Saturn*, the youngest Titan god; the Greek Kronos or Cronus
callidus, -a, -um - *clever, crafty*
gladius, -iī, m. - *sword*
oppugnō (1) - *to attack, assault*
sīc (adv.) - *so, thus*
imperium, -iī, n. - *power to command, supreme power, authority*

Grammar and Comprehension Questions

1) What tense, person, and number is *generāvērunt*?
2) What is unusual about the appearance of the Cyclopes?
3) How would you recognize the Giants? What, other than their size, is unusual about them?
4) Why did the Giants hate their father?
5) What form is *quod*? What is its grammatical function?
6) What case and function is *Ūranum*?

Gāia, māter terra, et Ūranus, pater caelum, in mātrimōniō
plūrimōs deōs **generāvērunt**. Gāia cum Ūranō generāvit duodecim
Tītānōs, sex deōs et sex deās. Cronus est minimus Tītānus. Rōmānī
Cronum Sāturnum vocābant. Gāia etiam multa mōnstra, Cyclōpēs
et Gigantēs, generāvit. Cyclōpēs erant validī et fulmen gubernābant,
sed sōlum ūnum oculum in frōnte habēbant. Trēs Gigantēs centum
brācchia et quīnquāgintā capita habēbant. Ūranus validōs fīliōs
timēbat. Gigantēs Ūranum ōdērunt, **quod** Ūranus puerōs in Gāiam
retrūdit. Gāia labōrābat et igitur suscēnsēbat. Callidus Sāturnus
Gāiam iuvāvit. **Ūranum** gladiō oppugnāvit et superāvit. Sīc Sāturnus
imperium habet.

Discussion Questions

1) The root *tītān-* has been used in a variety of ways. What words can you find that are derived from it?
2) James Lovelock, Dian Hitchcock, Lynn Margulis, and other modern scientists have formulated a Gaia principle in which the earth is itself a living, self-regulating being. How does this idea compare with the Hesiodic account? (See James Lovelock, *Gaia: A New Look at Life on Earth*, 1979.)
3) What words can you find that are derived from Cronus?

Cultural Influences

Music: Haydn oratorio, *The Creation* (1797); overture "The Representation of Chaos"; Paul Winter Consort, *Missa Gaia/ Earth Mass* (1982).

Saturn

Chapter Three

THE BATTLE OF THE GODS

When Saturn overthrew the first generation of gods, he imprisoned them in the depths of the underworld. Then with his sister, the Titan Ops (Rhea in Greek), Saturn created the third generation of gods, known as the Olympians, about whom you read in the first chapter. This passage, again following the story in Hesiod's *Theogony* (453–506), tells how and why the Olympians came to power.

rēgnō (1) - *to rule*
Ops, Opis, f. - *Ops, the Greek Rhea*
Rhea, -ae, f. - *Rhea*
lingua, -ae, f. - *language*
arcānum, -ī, n. - *secret*
narrō (1) - *to tell, narrate*
rēgnum, -ī, n. - *rule, kingdom*
5 vorō (1) - *to swallow, devour*
quotiēns (adv.) - *as often as, whenever*
īnfāns, -antis, m./f. - *infant, child*
lūgeō, -ēre, lūxī, lūctum - *to mourn, lament*
suscēnseō, -ēre, -uī - *to be angry*
ultimus, -a, -um - *last, final*
cēlō (1) - *to hide, conceal*
saxum, -ī, n. - *rock, stone*

textum -ī, n. - *cloth*
vēlātus, -a, -um - *covered, wrapped*
īnsula, -ae, f. - *island*
Crēta, -ae, f. - *Crete, an island in the Mediterranean south of Greece*
10 clam (adv.) - *secretly, under cover*
adolēscō, -ere, -olēvī - *to become mature, grow up*
dēnique (adv.) - *at last, finally*
generō (1) - *to produce, create*
Hestia, -ae, f. - *Hestia, the goddess of the hearth*
medicāmentum, -ī, n. - *drug*
15 vomō, -ere, -uī, -itum - *to vomit, spew out*
ūnā (adv.) - *together*
Tartarus, -ī, m. - *Tartarus, the underworld*

Grammar and Comprehension Questions

1) What is the secret that Gaia tells Saturn?
2) What tense, person, and number is *vorābō*?
3) What is the subject of *superābunt*?
4) What case is *textō* and why?
5) What tense, person, and number is *venerāverant*?
6) How did Rhea deceive Cronus?

Nunc Sāturnus in caelō rēgnābat. Soror Ops (Rhea in linguā Graecā vocābātur) erat uxor rēgīnaque. Gāia magnum arcānum Sāturnō narrāvit: "Ūnus fīliōrum tē superābit et tum rēgnum habēbit." Sāturnus igitur fīliōs suōs timēbat et cōnsilium cōgitābat. "Meōs fīliōs **vorābō**. Tum mē non **superābunt**." Quotiēns Ops īnfantem   5
generābat, Sāturnus īnfantem vorāvit. Māter igitur lūgēbat et suscēnsēbat. Ops cōnsilium suum cōgitābat: "Ultimum puerum meum cēlābō. Prō puerō saxum **textō** vēlātum Sāturnō dabō." Tum Sāturnus saxum vorāvit, sed Ops īnfantem in īnsulā Crētā cēlāvit. Ibi ultimus īnfāns, Iuppiter, clam adolēscēbat. Dēnique Iuppiter   10
iuvāre frātrēs suōs et sorōrēs cupiēbat. Nam Sāturnus et rēgīna sex deōs—trēs puellās, trēs puerōs—generāverant: Hestiam, Cererem, Iūnōnem, Plūtōnem, Neptūnum, et ultimum Iovem. Rōmānī hōs deōs Olympiōs vocābant. Iuppiter Sāturnō medicāmentum dedit. Tum Sāturnus saxum et aliōs Olympiōs deōs vomuit. Olympiī deī   15
contrā Sāturnum et Tītānōs bellum ūnā gerēbant. Iuppiter Cyclōpēs et Gigantēs ā Tartarō līberāvit.

Discussion Questions

1) What kind of parent is Saturn?
2) What sort of drug do you think Jupiter gave to Saturn? What do we call such a drug?
3) How does Jupiter treat the Cyclopes and Giants? How does this compare to Saturn's treatment of them?

sīc (adv.) - *so, thus*
tēlum, -ī, n. - *weapon*
plūrimus, -a, -um - *very many*
iactō (1) - *to throw, hurl*
20 pugna, -ae, f. - *fight*
imperium, -iī, n. - *power to command, supreme power, authority*
dīvidō, -ere, -vīsī, -vīsum - *to divide, distribute*
maximus, -a, -um - *greatest*
īnferī, -ōrum, m. pl. - *the dead*
vinculum, -ī, n. - *chain*
pōnō, -ere, posuī, positum - *to place, put*

Sāturnum nōn esse: accusative noun in indirect statement (see Wheelock, Ch. 25). Translate *esse* "was."
ad occidentem: *to the setting (sun), in the west*
25 aureus, -a, -um - *golden*
aevum -ī, n. - *age*
quotannīs (adv.) - *yearly*
in honōrem: with genitive, *in honor of*
fēriae, -ārum, f. pl. - *religious festival, holy day, holiday*
Sāturnālia, -ōrum, n. pl. - *the Saturnalia*, a festival in honor of Saturn on December 17

Grammar and Comprehension Questions

1) How did Jupiter get his weapon, the thunderbolt?
2) What are the principal parts of the verb from which *vicērunt* comes?
3) What type of pronoun is *sē*? To whom does it refer here?
4) Where are the Titans now?

Cyclōpēs Iovī fulmen dedērunt. Sīc fulmen est tēlum Iovis. Gigantēs centum manibus plūrima saxa dē monte Olympō iactābant. Sīc post longum bellum Olympiī Tītānōs māgnā pugnā **vīcērunt**. Trēs Olympiī frātrēs imperium inter **sē** dīvīsērunt. Tum Iuppiter maximus caelum, Neptūnus pontum, Plūtō īnferōs in Tartarō rēgnābat. Olympiī etiam Tītānōs in vincula in Tartarō posuērunt. Sed Rōmānī cōgitābant Sāturnum nōn esse in Tartarō. Sāturnus mortālēs ad occidentem in aureō aevō rēgnābat. Quotannīs Rōmānī in honōrem Sāturnī magnās fēriās, Sāturnālia, habēbant.

Discussion Questions

1) In the passage there are different viewpoints regarding the fate of Cronus/Saturn. What does this tell you about mythology?
2) What do you think Jupiter might fear threatens his power?
3) Investigate the Roman Saturnalia. What happened during the festival?

Titans

Cultural Influences

Art: Drawing by Peter Paul Rubens, *The Fall of the Titans* (c. 1635); drawing with watercolor by William Blake, *Hyperion driving out the forces of night* (1797–98); painting by Francisco Goya, *Cronus devouring one of his children* (1819–23).

Literature: poems entitled *Hyperion* by John Keats (incomplete, 1819) whose theme is the battle of the Titans; also Henry Wadsworth Longfellow (1839) and Algernon Swinburne (1859).

Goya's *Cronus devouring one of his children*

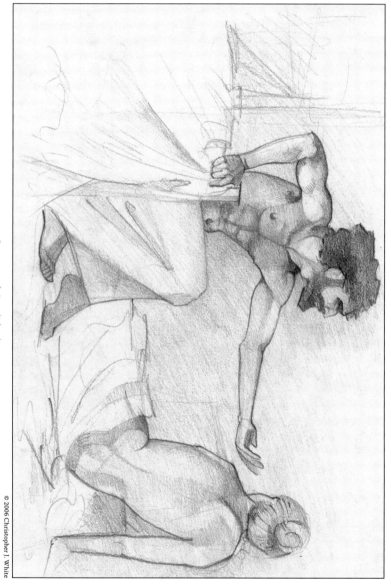

Saturn and Ops (Rhea)

Chapter Four

Prometheus: Inventor and Benefactor; Pandora

The origin of human beings has been a source of speculation in all cultures. In ancient Greece and Rome there were several co-existing explanations. In some, earth herself created man; in others, man was created by the gods. In Ovid we find an amalgamation of these two: the Titan Prometheus molded man from earth, which still retained celestial seeds and thus animated the new creature.

Prometheus, whose name means "fore-thought," knew the outcome of the battle between the Olympian gods and the Titans. Therefore, together with his brother Epimetheus ("after-thought"), he fought on the side of the Olympians. In many versions Prometheus was then entrusted with the task of creating man. Soon, however, Jupiter was displeased with this creation and wanted to destroy it. Prometheus pitied his creation and through his many gifts became the greatest benefactor of humans. His gifts, however, came at a cost both to himself and man. These costs will be examined more closely in the next chapters.

This reading initially follows the Ovidian version of man's creation. The passage then describes Prometheus' actions on behalf of mankind. The sources for this second section are Hesiod and the tragic poet Aeschylus.

Sources

Hesiod, *Works and Days* 42–105; *Theogony* 507–616 • Aeschylus, *Prometheus Bound* 107–12, 233–37, particularly 441–504 • Plato, *Protagoras* 321c8–322a3 • Vergil, *Georgics* 1.121–59 • Ovid, *Metamorphoses* 1. 76–88 • Apollodorus, *The Library* 1.vii.1

habitō (1) - *to live, dwell*
superius: neuter nominative singular adjective, *higher, superior*
ingenium, -iī, n. - *intelligence*
dēsum, -esse, -fuī, -futūrus - *to be missing, lacking*
nātus, -a, -um - *born*
fortasse (adv.) - *perhaps*
maximus, -a, -um - *greatest*
dīvīnus, -a, -um - *divine, sacred*
māteria, -ae, f. - *material, matter*
creō (1) - *to create*
vel (conj.) - *or*
Promētheus, -ī, m. - *Prometheus, a Titan; benefactor of mankind*
plēnā: takes genitive case
fōrmō (1) - *to form, shape, fashion*
5 **quamquam** (conj.) - *although*
cēterī, -ae, -a - *other*
prōnus, -a, -um - *prone, inclined forward*

spectō (1) - *to look at, see*
ērectus, -a, -um - *erect, upright*
levō (1) - *to raise, lift up*
sacrificō (1) - *to sacrifice*
miseria, -ae, f. - *misery, unhappiness, wretchness, distress*
optō (1) - *to desire, wish*
fraudō (1) - *to deceive, cheat*
sacrificium, -iī, n. - *sacrifice*
10 **inīquē** (adv.) - *unevenly*
dīvidō, -ere, -vīsī, -vīsum - *to divide, distribute*
os, ossis, n. - *bone*
sēbum, -ī, n. - *fat*
carō, carnis, m. - *meat*
stomachus, -ī, m. - *stomach*
vēlō (1) - *to conceal by covering, wrap*
ēligō, -ligere, -lēgī, -lēctum - *to choose, pick*

Grammar and Comprehension Questions

1) What person and number is *levāmus*?
2) What case is *hūmānīs* and what is its function?
3) How were humans suffering?
4) How did Prometheus deceive Jupiter?

Sacrificial procession in honor of Athena (Minerva)

Prometheus: Inventor and Benefactor; Pandora

Nunc terra erat, et ibi multa animālia habitābant. Sed superius animal magnō cum ingeniō dēerat. Tum homō nātus est. Fortasse maximus deus hūmānōs ē dīvīnā māteriā creāvit. Vel fortasse Promētheus ē terrā, plēnā dīvīnae māteriae, hūmānōs fōrmāvit. Quamquam cētera animālia prōna spectant terram, Promētheus hūmānōs ērectōs fōrmāvit. Quārē oculōs ad caelum **levāmus**.

Hūmānī animālia deīs sacrificābant, sed saepe parvus cibus erat **hūmānīs**. Promētheus hūmānam miseriam vidēbat et iuvāre optābat. Quārē Iovem fraudāre cōgitābat. Promētheus sacrificium inīquē dīvīsit. Ossa in sēbō, sed carnem in stomachō vēlābat. Promētheus Iovem vocāvit: "Potes eligere ūnum."

Discussion Questions

1) Are humans truly unique, or can other creatures look towards the sky?
2) Examine ancient sacrifice. What animal was normally sacrificed to Jupiter?

Suovetaurilia, Roman sacrifice of a pig, sheep, and bull

dolus, -ī, m. - *fraud, trick, deceit*
respondeō, -ēre, -spondī, -spōnsum - *to respond, answer, reply*
īrātus, -a, -um - *angered, angry*
malum, -ī, n. - *evil, misfortune*
cēlō (1) - *to hide, conceal*
ignis, -is, m. - *fire*
frīgidus, -a, -um - *cold, frigid*
15 coquō, -ere, coxī, coctum - *to cook*
iterum (adv.) - *again, a second time*
cavus, -a, -um - *hollow*
calamus, -ī, m. - *reed*
ferula, -ae, f. - *fennel, an herb*
portō (1) - *to carry*
dōnō: ablative of means, *because of...*
dissimilis, -e - *unlike, dissimilar*
20 Pandōra, -ae, f. - *Pandora, which means "all gifts" in Greek*
arca, -ae, f. - *box*
iubeō, -ēre, iūssī, iūssum - *to order, command*
Epimētheus, -ī, m. - *Epimetheus, "after-thought," brother of Prometheus*

accipiō, -ere, -cēpī, -ceptum - *to accept, receive*
reserō (1) - *to open*
nē (conj.) - *not;* with imperative, *do not*
25 mox (adv.) - *soon*
cūriōsus, -a, -um - *inquisitive, curious*
ēvolō (1) - *to fly out*
statim (adv.) - *immediately*
claudō, -ere, clausī, clausum - *to shut*
intus (adv.) - *within*
doleō, -ēre, -uī, -itum - *to grieve for*
30 tectum, -ī, n. - *shelter, house*
cognōscō, -ere, -nōvī, -nitum - *to get to know, know*
lingua, -ae, f. - *language*
nāvigātiō, -tiōnis, f. - *navigation*
praedictiō, -tiōnis, f. - *prophecy*
breviter (adv.) - *in short, briefly*

Grammar and Comprehension Questions

1) What tense, person and number is *dīvīsistī*?
2) How did Prometheus bring fire to earth?
3) What case is *dōnum*? What is its function?
4) What form is *reserā*?
5) What tense is *accipiēs*?
6) What "gift" did Zeus give man in return for Prometheus' theft?
7) What was left in the box?
8) What type of infinitives are *vīvere, cognōscere,* and *habēre*?

Iuppiter dolum vīdit et respondit: "Inīquē sacrificium **dīvīsistī**."
Tum Iuppiter īrātus ossa in sēbō ēlēgit et mala hūmānīs cōgitābat.
Iuppiter ignem ā hūmānīs cēlāvit. Hūmānī igitur erant frīgidī
neque cibum coquere poterant. Sed iterum Promētheus dolum 15
contrā Iovem cogitābat. Ignem in cavō calamō ferulae cēlāvit et ē
caelō ad terram portāvit. Tum ignem hūmānīs dedit.

Iuppiter dōnō ignis īrātus est. Dissimile **dōnum** hūmānīs dare
cogitābat. Volcānus bellam fēminam ē terrā creāvit. Deī deaeque
multa dōna fēminae dabant. Fēminam Pandōram vocābant. Iuppiter 20
etiam magnam arcam plēnam malōrum fēminae dabat. Iuppiter
Pandōram iubēbat: "Nē arcam **reserā**." Iuppiter fēminam cum arcā
Epimētheō dare optābat. Sed Promētheus frātrem Epimētheum
monuit: "Sī puellam **accipiēs**, hūmānī bene vīvere nōn poterunt."
Sed Epimētheus fēminam amābat et dōnum accēpit. Mox cūriōsa 25
Pandōra arcam reserāvit et multa mala vitiaque ēvolāvērunt. Statim
Pandōra arcam clausit. Spēs sōla intus remanēbat.

Tum Promētheus hūmānōs dolēbat. Spem ex arcā remōvit et
hūmānīs dedit. Promētheus etiam multa alia dōna hūmānīs dedit.
Docuit hūmānōs **vīvere** in tectīs, **cognōscere** tempora annī, et 30
linguam **habēre**. Agrī cultūra, medicīna, nāvigātiō, praedictiō sunt
dōna Promētheī. Breviter, Promētheus tōtam scientiam hūmānīs dedit.

Discussion Questions

1) Why would Jupiter find fat desirable? What might this tell us about the ancient diet?
2) How does this version of early mankind compare with the modern view? Do we believe in a Promethean figure?
3) Who is the biblical equivalent of Pandora? How do the stories compare?

Cultural Influences

Art: Roman Sarcophagus: "Prometheus, in the presence of the Olympian gods, creates man" (National Museum, Naples); Peter Paul Rubens, "Prometheus (with Fire)," painting (1636–38) and "Prometheus Bound" (1610–11); Paul Manship, "Prometheus," gilded bronze fountain figure carrying torch, Rockefeller Center, NYC (1933–34); Walter Crane, "Pandora opens the box" watercolor (1885); Auguste Rodin, "Vulcan Creating Pandora," bronze sculpture (1889); Odilon Redon, "Pandora," painting (1910).

Ballet: Ludwig von Beethoven, *The Creatures of Prometheus* (1801); Maurice Béjart, *Prométhée* (1956); Frederick Ashton, *The Creatures of Prometheus* (1970).

Literature: Mary Wollstonecraft Shelley, *Frankenstein, or the Modern Prometheus* (1817).

Music: cantata by Franz Schubert (1816); tone poem by Alexander Scriabin, *Prometheé: Le poeme du feu* (1908–10); operas by Gabriel Fauré, *Prométhée* (1900), Leoncavallo (1919), Orff (1968), and by Alban Berg, *Lulu (or a modern Pandora)* (1928–34).

Pandora releases evil into the world

Chapter Five

PROMETHEUS PUNISHED

Although Prometheus had helped Jupiter to achieve power, Jupiter bitterly resented Prometheus' theft of fire and the other benefits he bestowed on mankind. Prometheus' independent actions, as a threat to Jupiter's power, had to be punished. Therefore, Jupiter decided to imprison Prometheus as far from humanity as possible and to make him suffer for all time. This passage describes both the torments Prometheus suffered and how he was ultimately released. The final part of the story is based upon fragments from Aeschylus' lost play, *Prometheus Unbound*. Scholars are not sure whether Prometheus was released before or after he made a great revelation.

SOURCES

Hesiod, *Theogony* 521–34 • Aeschylus, *Prometheus Bound* • Lucian, *Dialogues of the Gods* 5 (Zeus and Prometheus)

īrātus, -a, -um - *angered, angry*
volēbat: *wished, was wanting*
statuō, -ere, -uī, -ūtum - *to decide*
aeternus, -a, -um - *eternal*
multō (1) - *to punish*
5 abstulerat: *had stolen*
iubeō, -ēre, iussī, iussum - *to order, command*
ligō (1) - *to bind, fasten*
vinculum, -ī, n. - *chain*
Caucasus, -ī, m. - *the Caucasus, a mountain range between the Black and Caspian Seas*
invītus, -a, -um - *unwilling*
rūpēs, -is, f. – *steep, rocky cliff; crag*
saevus, -a, -um - *harsh, savage, cruel*
famulus, -ī, m. - *servant, attendant*
cōgō, -ere, coēgī, coāctum - *to compel*
sudis, -is, f. - *stake*
pectus, -toris, n. - *chest*
pellō, -ere, pepulī, pulsum - *to strike, drive*
sileō, -ēre, -uī - *to be silent*
cum: here, *when*
absum, -esse, -fuī, -futūrus - *to be absent, away*
dēnique (adv.) - *at last, finally*

10 plōrō (1) - *to utter a cry of grief or pain*
Ōceanītis, -tidis, f. - *Oceanid, minor goddess, daughter of Ocean*
vōx, vōcis, f. - *voice, word*
adventō (1) - *to approach*
rogō (1) - *to ask*
tam (adverb used to intensify adjective) - *so*
respondeō, -ēre, -spondī, -spōnsum - *to respond, answer, reply*
15 voluntās, -tātis, f. - *will, wish*
ut (conj.) - *as*

20 etiamnum (adv.) - *still, even now*
aquila, -ae, f. - *eagle*
cruciō (1) - *to torture, torment*
cōtīdiē (adv.) - *daily*
iecur, iecoris, n. - *liver (considered to be the source of emotions)*
carpō, -ere, carpsī, carptum - *to pluck at*
vorō (1) - *to eat greedily, swallow, devour*
nox, noctis, f. - *night*
cōnsānēscō, -ere, -uī - *to heal up, be healed*

Grammar and Comprehension Questions

1) What case is *hominibus?* What is its function?
2) What tense, person and number is *audēbam?* What are its principal parts?
3) Identify the form *dā*.
4) What power does Prometheus have over Jupiter, despite his bondage?
5) What additional punishment did Jupiter give Prometheus?

Iuppiter īrātus erat quod Promētheus ignem **hominibus** dederat.
Iuppiter Promētheum necāre volēbat, sed Promētheus immortālis
erat. Iuppiter igitur statuit Promētheum, prō amōre hominum, in
aeternum tempus multāre. Quod Promētheus ignem Volcānī
abstulerat, Iuppiter iūssit Volcānum ligāre Promētheum vinculīs. 5
In Caucasō, terrā remōtā ab hominibus, invītus Volcānus
Promētheum ad rūpem ligāvit. Saevī famulī Iovis Volcānum
cōgēbant. Tum Volcānus sudem per pectus Promētheī pepulit.
Promētheus silēbat. Cum Volcānus famulīque aberant, dēnique
Promētheus plōrābat. Mox Ōceanītidēs vōcem audīvērunt et 10
adventāvērunt. Rogāvērunt: "Cūr tam saevam poenam tolerās?
Quis tē vinculīs ligāvit?" Promētheus respondit: "Rēx deōrum
Volcānum iūssit mē ligāre. Ignem et alia dōna hominibus dare
audēbam. Sed nōn in aeternum tempus poenam tolerābō. Post
multum tempus magnus vir mē līberābit." Fēminae rogāvērunt: 15
"Cūr? Quī vir audēbit tē līberāre contrā voluntātem Iovis?"
Promētheus respondit: "Sēcrētum sciō. Sī Iuppiter certam
fēminam amābit, illa fēmina fīlium creābit. Tum ille fīlius Iovem
superābit, ut Iuppiter patrem Sāturnum superāvit." Ōceanītidēs
respondērunt: "Nōmen fīliī nōbīs **dā**." Promētheus dīxit: "Nōn 20
possum. Sēcrētum meum mē līberābit. Sine sēcrētō hanc poenam
semper tolerābō." Iuppiter, etiamnum īrātus, aquilam iūssit
Promētheum cruciāre. Cōtīdiē aquila iecur Promētheī carpēbat
vorābatque. Nocte iecur cōnsanēscēbat.

Discussion Questions

1) Why was it Vulcan whom Jupiter ordered to punish Prometheus?
2) Why did Jupiter choose the Caucasus as Prometheus' place of punishment?

25 **prīmus, -a, -um** - *first*
lūx, lūcis, f. - *light, day*
rursum (adv.) - *again*
etiam (adv.) - *also, even*
frīgeō, -ēre - *to be cold*
diē: ablative of time when, *in the day*
calor, -lōris, m. - *warmth, heat*
vexō (1) - *to ravage, afflict*
dīvulgō (1) - *to reveal, divulge*
Nērēis, -ēidis, f. - *a Nereid*, a sea-nymph
Thetis, -idis, f. - *Thetis*, a Nereid, mother of Achilles
Pēleus, -ī, m. - *Peleus*, king of Phthia, father of Achilles

nūbō, -ere, nūpsī, nūptum (+ dat.) - *to marry*
posteā (adv.) - *afterwards*
Achillēs, -is, m. - *Achilles*, son of Peleus and Thetis, Greek hero of the Trojan war
30 **propitius, -a, -um** - *favorably inclined, well-disposed, propitious*
grātus, -a, -um - *grateful*
venia, -ae, f. - *pardon, forgiveness*
Herculēs, -is, m. - *Hercules*, the Greek Heracles, son of Jupiter/Zeus and the mortal Alcmena
sagitta, -ae, f. - *arrow*
iterum (adv.) - *again, a second time*

Grammar and Comprehension Questions

1) What case is *prīmā lūce?* Why?
2) What word contrasts with *nocte?*
3) How long did Prometheus remain in bondage?
4) What type of ablative construction is *cum deīs?*

Vulcan

Tum **prīmā lūce** aquila hoc rursum vorābat. Etiam **nocte** 25
Promētheus frīgēbat; diē calor sōlis corpus vexābat.

Post multa mīlia annōrum Promētheus sēcrētum dīvulgāvit.
Fēmina erat Nērēis, Thetis. Iuppiter tum Thetidem iūssit mortālī
vīrō, Pēleō, nūbere. Posteā Thetis fīlium Achillem generāvit.
Iuppiter, nunc propitius et grātus, veniam Promētheō dedit. Tum 30
Herculēs, fīlius Iovis, aquilam sagittā necāvit et Promētheum ē
vinculīs līberāvit. Promētheus iterum **cum deīs** habitābat.

Discussion Questions

1) Why does the eagle particularly attack the liver? What association did the liver have?
2) The attendants of Jupiter are named Might and Force (*Kratos* and *Bia* in Greek). What do we learn in this passage about the nature of Jupiter's early rule?
3) What does the fact that Prometheus knows a secret about Jupiter tell us about Jupiter? Do the ancient Greeks and Romans consider him to be omniscient?
4) Can you think of a figure who is equivalent to Prometheus in his suffering?
5) Carefully examine the words in the passage. How many English words can you find that derive from the Latin words?

The eagle attacks Prometheus' liver

Cultural Influences

Art: Peter Paul Rubens painting, *Prometheus Bound* (1610–11) and John Singer Sargeant painting of Prometheus on ceiling of rotunda, Museum of Fine Arts, Boston (1921).

Literature: Percy Bysshe Shelley, *Prometheus Unbound*, dramatic poem (1820); Franz Kafka, *Prometheus*, novella (1917).

Music: symphonic poem by Franz Lizst, *Prometheus* (1850), based on text of Johann Gottfried von Herder's dramatic poem, *The Freeing of Prometheus* (1802); operas by Gabriel Fauré (1900) and Carl Orff (1968).

For additional references and discussion of the Prometheus and Pandora themes in authors such as Spenser, Milton, Byron, Goethe, Longfellow, Melville, Gidé, Lowell, and Bridges, see Philip Mayerson, *Classical Mythology in Literature, Art, and Music* (Glenview, Ill.: Scott, Foresman & Co., 1971), pp. 45–54.

Prometheus in chains

Prometheus' Liver Eaten by the Eagle

Chapter Six

THE AGES OF MAN

The Greeks and Romans believed that man had undergone a process of degeneration from an early, idyllic state of close communication with the gods, which they called the Golden Age, to the present state of human sinfulness, which they called the Iron Age. The degeneration was caused by increasing human immorality. The Greek epic poet Hesiod, our first source, believed there were five ages of man: gold, silver, bronze, the age of heroes, and iron. Many centuries later Ovid reduced this number to four by omitting the age of heroes. Vergil in the *Georgics* viewed the degeneration in a somewhat more positive light. In a passage termed Jupiter's theodicy Vergil claimed that Jupiter intentionally ended the Golden Age and made life more difficult for humans in order that man might ennoble himself. As a result man left behind his Golden Age sloth and developed the arts and civilization.

The passage below is drawn primarily from the accounts in Hesiod and Ovid. It also includes some Vergilian and Horatian phraseology.

SOURCES

Hesiod, *Works and Days* 106–201 • Pindar, *Second Olympian Ode* 61–83 • Vergil, *Georgics* 1. 118–159 • Ovid, *Metamorphoses* 1. 89–150

OTHER PASSAGES OF INTEREST

Homer in *Odyssey* 4. 561–69 speaks briefly of an idyllic place he calls Elysion, the islands of the blessed. Those specially favored by the gods will live there forever. The language of the passage prefigures the Golden Age description of Hesiod. Also, in *Odyssey* 7.112–132 the description of the island of the Phaeacians contains numerous golden age elements.

Vergil in *Eclogues* 4 predicts a return to the Golden Age coincident with the birth of a child.

Ovid, in describing the original golden age in the *Metamorphoses*, echoes Vergil's phraseology.

Horace in *Epodes* 16, despairing of the corrupt situation at Rome, issues a call to migrate to the west where they can establish a new golden age (41–66).

There is also an opposing view in Lucretius, *De rerum natura* 5. 925–1457. Lucretius argues that man by trial and error gradually discovered fire, clothing, and other necessities. The life of early man was difficult and humans were physically hardier. Then, as they developed civilization, they gradually softened. In this view there is no Promethean figure nor any golden age. On the other hand, Lucretius points out that through appreciation of simple pleasures early man may have enjoyed himself more than people today, who are corrupted by materialism.

Sumerian mythology also depicts a paradise called Dilmun, a garden rich with fruits, fields, and meadows. Although Dilmun seems to have been for gods, not mortals, its imagery has influenced the depiction of Eden in the Bible.

---

aureus, -a, -um - *golden*
prīmus, -a, -um - *first*
coāctus, -a, -um - *compelled, forced*
pietās, -tātis, f. - *dutifulness, respectfulness, piety*
exerceō, -ēre, -uī, -itum - *to practice, exercise, perform*
absum, -esse, -fuī, -futūrus - *to be absent, missing*
dēscendō, -ere, -scendī, -scēnsum - *to descend*
ignōrō (1) - *to have no knowledge of, be ignorant or unaware of*
similis (+ dat.) - *like*
5 **somnus, -ī, m.** - *sleep*
vōmer, -meris, m. - *plowshare, plow*
cōpiōsus, -a, -um - *abundant, plentiful*
cibus, -ī, m. - *food*
vēr, vēris, n. - *spring (the season)*
lac, lactis, n. - *milk*

flāvus, -a, -um - *yellow, golden-colored*
mel, mellis, n. - *honey*
arbor, -boris, f. - *tree*
mānō (1) - *to flow, drip*
serpēns, -pentis, m. - *serpent, snake*
adsum, -esse, -fuī, -futūrus - *to be present*
iniūssus, -a, -um - *not ordered, unbidden*
grex, gregis, m. - *herd, flock*
mulctrum, -ī, n. - *milking pail*
leō, leōnis, m. - *lion*
metuō, -ere, -uī - *to fear*
pereō, -īre, -iī, -itum - *to perish, die*
anima, -ae, f. - *soul, spirit*
10 **malum, -ī, n.** - *evil*
super (prep. + acc.) - *upon*
prōtegō, -ere, -tēxī, -tēctum - *to protect, defend against*

Grammar and Comprehension Questions

1) What does *coactī* modify?
2) What tense is *periit*?
3) What word is *hōrum*? What is its gender, number, and case?
4) What case is *hominēs*?
5) What was earth like during the Golden Age? How was it different from today?
6) What happened to the souls of Golden Age people?

Aurea erat prīma aetās. Hominēs in pāce vīvēbant; nōn **coāctī**
pietātem exercēbant. Poena metusque aberant. Deī ad terram
dēscendēbant et cum hominibus cēnābant. Hominēs senectūtem
et morbum ignōrābant. Post multum tempus mors erat similis
somnō. Terra ipsa sine vōmere cōpiōsum cībum hominibus per   5
sē dabat. Vēr erat aeternum. Flūmina lactis fluēbant; flāvum mel
dē arboribus mānābat. Nūllus serpēns aderat. Iniūssī gregēs ad
mulctra currēbant. Gregēs leōnēs nōn metuēbant. Dēnique aureum
genus hominum **periit**. Tamen animae **hōrum** etiam nunc super
terram sunt et **hominēs** ā malō prōtegunt.   10

Discussion Questions

1) Compare the description of the Golden Age with Eden in the Bible.
2) What sort of foods did earth provide during this age?

postquam (conj.) - *after*
vī: ablative, *by force, necessity*
argenteus, -a, -um - *of silver*
dēterior: nominative singular feminine adjective, *worse, inferior*
exsistō, -ere, -stitī, -stitum - *to arise, come forth, come into existence*
annus, -ī, m. - *year*
adōlēscō, -ere, -lēvī - *to grow up*
domī: *at home*
lūdō, -ere, lūsī, lūsum - *to play*
adultus, -a, -um - *full-grown, mature*
breviter (adv.) - *for a short time, briefly*
miseria, -ae, f. - *misery, unhappiness, wretchedness*
15 **colō, -ere, coluī, cultum** - *to worship*
terminō (1) - *to end, conclude*
fervidus, -a, -um - *intensely hot, blazing*

aestās, -tātis, f. - *summer*
frīgidus, -a, -um - *cold, frigid*
hiems, -mis, f. - *winter*
addō, -ere, -didī, -ditum - *to add*
prīmum (adv.) - *for the first time*
petō, -ere, -īvī, -ītum - *to seek*
perdō, -ere, -didī, -ditum - *to destroy*
aēneus, -a, -um - *of bronze*
20 **membrum, -ī, n.** - *limb*
arma, -ōrum, n. pl. - *arms, weapons*
saevus, -a, -um - *harsh, savage, cruel*
Mars, Martis, m. - *Mars, god of war, the Greek Ares*
exerceō, -ēre, -uī, -itum - *to practice, use*
pānis, -is, m. - *bread*
proelium, -iī, n. - *battle*

Grammar and Comprehension Questions

1) Where did Saturn go?
2) How did Jupiter change the earth in creating the Silver Age?
3) What case is the phrase *aēnea arma?* Is it subject or direct object?
4) What is the understood subject of *exercēbant* and *ignōrābant?*

Postquam Sāturnus in Tartarum vī dēscendit, Iuppiter erat rēx.
Tum argentea aetās, dēterior aetās exstitit. Puerī centum annōs
adōlēscēbant et cum mātribus domī lūdēbant. **Adultī** sōlum
breviter et in miseriā vīvēbant. Nam sine pietāte sē gerēbant. Dēos
nōn colēbant; deīs nōn sacrificābant. Tum Iuppiter aeternum vēr   15
termināvit. Fervidam aestātem et frīgidam hiemem addidit. Tum
prīmum hominēs tecta petēbant et in agrīs labōrābant. Dēnique
Iuppiter argenteum genus perdidit.

Tertium genus erat aēneum. Hominēs erant validī magnīs
membrīs. **Aēnea arma** saevī Martis **exercēbant**. Pānem **ignōrābant**.   20
Dēnique sē in proeliō dēlēbant et in Tartarum dēscendēbant.

Discussion Questions

1) Do you see an inconsistency in the life spans in the traditional description of the Silver Age?
2) What was the main characteristic of the Silver Age that offended the gods?

Etruscan statuette of Mars

hērōicus, -a, -um - *heroic*
animōsus, -a, -um - *spirited, bold, courageous*
iūstus, -a, -um - *just*
sēmideus, -ī, m. - *demi-god, half-god*
ut (conj.) - *as, like*
Achillēs, -is, m. - *Achilles,* son of Peleus and Thetis, Greek hero of the Trojan war
Ulixēs, -is, m. - *Ulysses,* the Greek Odysseus, king of Ithaca
Trōiānus, -a, -um - *Trojan*
iūssū: ablative, *by order of*
īnsula, -ae, f. - *island*
solūtus, -a, -um - *freed*
25 **frūx, frūgis, f.** - *fruit, crops*

ter (adv.) - *three times, thrice*
effundō, -ere, -fūdī, -fūsum - *to pour out, forth*
ultimus, -a, -um - *last, final*
ferreus, -a, -um - *iron, of iron*
cessō (1) - *to stop, cease*
vexō (1) - *to ravage, afflict, harry*
messis, -is, f. - *harvest*
dissideō, -ēre, -ēdī - *to disagree, differ*
30 **superbia, -ae, f.** - *arrogance, pride*
iūstitia, -ae, f. - *justice*
pudor, -dōris, m. - *shame, modesty*
hospes, -pitis, m. - *guest; host;* both meanings occur here.
tūtus, -a, -um - *safe*

Grammar and Comprehension Questions

1) What war took place during the Age of Heroes?
2) What noun must you understand with *multī*?
3) Why is the last age called the Iron Age? What was made of iron?
4) What tense is *neglegent*?
5) What English words are derived from Saturn?

Quārta aetās erat hēroica, in proeliō animōsa sed etiam iūsta. Graecī hōs sēmideōs vocābant, ut Achillem Ulixemque. **Multī** in Trōiānō bellō periērunt. Paucī, iūssū Iovis, in beātīs īnsulīs sub solūtō Sāturnō habitant. Ibi terra frūgēs ter in annō effundit. 25
Ultima aetās, nostra aetās, est ferrea. Nunc labōrāre numquam cessāmus. Terram in agrōs dīvidimus et vōmeribus vexāmus, sed terra parvam messem saepe dat. Deī multa mala sed etiam pauca bona hominibus dant. Mox pater et puerī dissidēbunt. Ūna urbs aliam urbem dēlēbit. Hominēs pietātem **neglegent** et superbiam malumque laudābunt. 30
Iustitia erit vīs; pudor fidēsque nōn erunt. Hospes ab hospite nōn erit tūtus; frāter ā frātrō nōn erit tūtus. Tum Iuppiter nostrum genus dēlēbit.

Discussion Questions

1) Compare the depiction of the Golden Age with that of Eden in the Bible (*Genesis* 2).
2) Compare the description of the future of the Iron Age with the biblical version of Armageddon (*Revelations* 16).
3) If not iron, what would you call the age in which you now live?

Cultural Influences

Literature: Edmund Spenser in *Fairie Queen*, Book 5 speaks of a Golden Age under the rule of Saturn (c. 1590), and Percy Bysshe Shelley in his poem *Epipsychidion* 422–512 speaks of an Edenic isle in the Aegean (1821).

Music: Thea Musgrave, *The Five Ages of Man*, piece for chorus and orchestra (1963).

Chapter Seven

THE FLOOD: DEUCALION AND PYRRHA

The story of a great flood that destroyed all mankind except a chosen few seems nearly universal in the human imagination. Although the details vary, there is remarkable overall consistency in the stories. The Sumerian *Epic of Gilgamesh* records the story of king Gilgamesh living in about 2700 BC (the written version dates from about 700 BC). Utnapishtim, a good man, tells the king how he survived a great flood caused by the water god to destroy man. Forewarned by the goddess of wisdom, he survived the flood by building a boat in which he stored seeds, animals, and his family. After a week-long storm, the ship grounded on a mountain, and he released birds to look for land. The biblical version that features Noah is probably the most familiar. In the Greco-Roman version, Jupiter is angered by the immorality and arrogance of man and decides to destroy the race by causing a great flood. Once again Prometheus assists mankind. He tells his son Deucalion and his wife Pyrrha (the child of Epimetheus and Pandora), who are both renowned for piety, to build a ship. Ovid vividly describes the tremendous flood and storm. Then he turns to the desperation of the couple who are the only survivors. They appeal for divine aid to restore the human race. A puzzling prophecy brings about the surprising repopulation of the world. This passage is drawn primarily from Ovid's *Metamorphoses* 1.277–415.

SOURCES

The Epic of Gilgamesh Tablet 11 • Pindar, *Oympian Ode* 9.41–56 • Bible, Genesis 6.5–6 • Ovid, *Metamorphoses* 1.177–415 • Apollodorus, *The Library* 1.vii.2

superbus, -a, -um - *arrogant, overbearing, haughty, proud*
adōrō (1) - *to worship*
dēcernō, -ere, -crēvī, -crētum - *to decide*
imber, -bris, m. - *rain*
ēmittō, -ere, -mīsī, -missum - *to send out, release, let fly*
ruō, -ere, ruī - *to rush, fall, be ruined*
discrīmen, -minis, n. - *difference, distinction*
5 **undique** (adv.) - *on all sides, everywhere*
collis, -is, m. - *hill, hill-top*
occupō (1) - *to take up, fill, occupy*
cumba, -ae, f. - *small boat, skiff*
sedeō, -ēre, sēdī, sessum - *to sit*
rēmus, -ī, m. - *oar*
ducit: here, *plies, uses*
illic (adv.) - *at that place, there*
arō (1) - *to plow*
piscis, -is, m. - *fish*

delphīnus, -ī, m. - *dolphin*
silva, -ae, f. - *forest*
dēspērātus, -a, -um - *desperate, hopeless*
ūnā (adv.) - *together*
natō (1) - *to swim*
lupus, -ī, m. - *wolf*
ovis, -is, f. - *sheep*
avis, -is, f. - *bird*
rāmus, -ī, m. - *bough, branch, twig*
postrēmō (adv.) - *finally*
Deucaliōn, -ōnis, m. - *Deucalion, son of Prometheus; king in region of Greece*
Pyrrha, -ae, f. - *Pyrrha, daughter of Epimetheus and Pandora; wife of Deucalion*
10 **dīluvium, -iī, n.** *flood, deluge*
melior: nominative singular masculine adjective, *better*
magis (adv.) - *more*
metuō, -ere, -uī - *to revere*

Grammar and Comprehension Questions

1) To what does *hōs* refer?
2) To whom do *hic* and *ille* refer?
3) What gender, number and case is *omnia*?
4) How is *dē* translated?
5) What were the special characteristics of Deucalion and Pyrrha?
6) How were Deucalion and Pyrrha related?

Hominēs nimis superbī erant et deōs nōn adōrābant. Iuppiter
igitur dēlēre **hōs** dēcrēvit. Ipse plūrimum imbrem ēmittēbat.
Etiam Neptūnum iubēbat ēmittere flūmina mareque. Tum flūmina
per agrōs ruēbant. Nunc mare et terra nūllum discrīmen habēbant.
Aqua undique erat. **Hic** collem occupat, **ille** in cumbā sedet et 5
rēmōs illic dūcit, ubi nūper arābat. Piscēs et delphīnī silvās tenent.
Dēspērāta animālia ūnā natant, lupī inter ovēs. Etiam avēs nūllum
rāmum invenīre possunt. Postrēmō aqua **omnia** necat. Sed
Promētheus fīlium suum, Deucaliōnem, et uxōrem eius, Pyrrham,
dē dīluviō monuerat. Nūllus vir erat melior; nūlla fēmina deōs 10
magis metuēbat.

Discussion Questions

1) Can you think of a word to describe this sort of world-ending disaster?
2) Jupiter's intent was to destroy the human race. What do you think happened to the animals?

Neptune with trident

aedificō (1) - *to build, construct*
pāreō, -ēre, -uī (+ dat.) - *to obey*
accidō, -ere, -cidī - *to happen*
Parnāsus, -ī, m. - *Parnasus, a mountain in Greece, near Delphi*
suprēmus, -a, -um - *highest*

15 adhaereō, -ēre, -haesī, -haesum - *to stick to, adhere*
relinquō, -ere, -līquī, -lictum - *to leave behind, leave*
ambō, ambae, ambō - *both*
innocuus, -a, -um - *innocent, blameless*
tot (indecl. adj.) - *so many*
supersum, -esse, -fuī, -futūrus - *to remain*
superesse: infinitive in indirect statement (see Wheelock, Ch. 25); translate *were remaining, were left*
orbis, -is, m. - *circle*; orbis terrārum: *the world, the earth*
pius, -a, -um - *pious, faithful*
revocō (1) - *to call back, recall*

20

habēret: imperfect tense, subjunctive mood (see Wheelock, Ch. 29), *held, had*
vīvō, -ere, vīxī, vīctum - *to live*
nōllem: imperfect tense, subjunctive mood in condition (see Wheelock, Ch. 33), *I would not wish*
Themis, -is, f. - *Themis, ancient goddess associated with Gaia, with justice, and with prophecy*
accēdō, -ere, -cessī, -cessum - *to come near, approach*
muscus, -ī, m. - *moss*
palleō, -ēre - *to be pale, discolored, yellowish*
āra, -ae, f. - *altar*
prōnus, -a, -um - *lying on the ground, prone*

25 prex, precis, f. - *prayer*
quōmodo (adv.) - *how, in what way*
restituō, -ere, -uī, -ūtum - *to replace, restore*
sors, -rtis, f. - *oracular response, prophecy*

Grammar and Comprehension Questions

1) What form is *aedificāte*?
2) What case is *aquā* and what is its function?
3) What is the subject of *remōvit*?
4) What case is *uxor*?
5) Why did Jupiter finally stop the storms and floods?
6) Why were Deucalion and Pyrrha chosen to be the survivors?
7) How did the flood affect Themis' temple?

Promētheus iūsserat: "Nāvem **aedificāte**, quod Iuppiter orbem
terrārum **aquā** dēlēbit." Patrī pārēbant. Mox illud dīluvium accidit.
Post multum tempus nāvis illōrum in Parnāsō, suprēmō monte,
adhaesit. Deucaliōn Pyrrhaque nāvem relīquērunt et deōs adōrābant. 15
Tum Iuppiter vidēbat illum ūnum virum et illam ūnam fēminam,
ambōs innocuōs, dē tot mīlibus superesse. Iuppiter igitur īram contrā
hominēs āmīsit et hōs duōs piōs vīvere permīsit. Tum imbrōs et
nūbēs **remōvit**. Neptūnus aquās revocāvit.
Deucaliōn Pyrrhae dīxit: "Ō **uxor**, fēmina sōla es. Nunc perīcula 20
nōs iungunt. In tōtā terrā sōlī sumus. Sī tē quoque māre habēret,
vīvere nōllem. Pater meus hominēs ē terrā aquāque creāvit. Sed hoc
gerere nōn possumus." Tum ad templum deae Themis accēdēbant.
Templum muscō pallēbat; āra sine igne erat. Prōnī dīcēbant: "Sī
precēs deōs movent, Themis, nōs iuvā. Dā cōnsilium. Quōmodo 25
hūmānum genus restituēmus?" Dea hanc sortem dedit:

Discussion Question

1) Investigate Mt. Parnasus. What other associations does it have?
2) Investigate the goddess Themis. What is her relationship to Prometheus? What are her functions?

vēlō (1) - *to conceal by covering, veil*
vestis, -is, f. - *clothing*
resolvō, -ere, -solvī, -solūtum - *to loosen, untie*
os, ossis, n. - *bone*
parēns, -rentis, m./f. - *parent*
tergum, -ī, n. - *back*
iactō (1) - *to throw, hurl*
obstupēscō, -ere, -stupuī - *to be astounded, struck dumb*
recūsō (1) - *to refuse*
venia, -ae, f. - *pardon, forgiveness*
rogō (1) - *to ask, ask for*
30   falsus, -a, -um - *false, deceptive*
fortasse (adv.) - *perhaps*

lapis, -pidis, m. - *stone*
dubius, -a, -um - *doubtful, uncertain*
iniūria, -ae, f. - *injustice, injury, wrong*
dīvīnitus (adv.) - *divinely, by divine means*
mollēscō, -ere - *to become soft*
crēscō, -ere, crēvī, crētum - *to increase, grow*
iactātus, -a, -um - *having been thrown, hurled*

35

dūrus, -a, -um - *hard, harsh, rough, hardy*
dūrō (1) - *to endure*

Grammar and Comprehension Questions

1) What does Pyrrha refuse to do?
2) What gender, number, and case is *falsae*? What does it modify?
3) What case does *in* take here? How is it translated?
4) Why is the human race tough?

"Discēdite ē templō et vēlāte capita. Vestēs resolvite. Ossa magnae parentis post terga iactāte!" Deucaliōn Pyrrhaque obstupēscēbant. Pia Pyrrha deae pārēre recūsābat, sed veniam rogābat. Tum Deucalion cōgitāvit: "Sortēs deae numquam **falsae** sunt. Fortasse magna parēns est terra ipsa. Ossa sunt lapidēs terrae ipsīus. Themis nōs iubet lapidēs post terga iactāre." Pyrrha dubia erat, sed nūllam iniūriam in hōc vidēbat. Lapidēs post terga iactāvērunt. Dīvīnitus hī lāpidēs mollescēbant et crēscēbant **in** fōrmās hominum. Lapidēs iactātī ā Deucaliōne mox erant virī, lapidēs iactātī ā Pyrrhā erant fēminae. Quod ē lapidibus sumus, genus dūrum sumus et labōrem dūrāmus. 30

35

DISCUSSION QUESTIONS

1) Compare the Ovidian version of the flood with those in *The Epic of Gilgamesh* and *The Bible*. What similarities and differences do you find?
2) In *The Bible* to whom are Decualion and Pyrrha equivalent? How close is the comparison?
3) For further information on this theme see *The Flood Myth*, ed. Alan Dundes (Berkeley: University of California Press, 1988), a collection of writings from various disciplinary perspectives which analyze flood myths throughout the world. In addition to the stories noted above, there is a Mesopotamian myth about a flood survivor, Atrahasis; the Irish legend of Queen Cesair who sailed for about seven years when oceans overwhelmed Ireland; also American Indian legends.
4) Later in the *Metamorphoses* (8.618–724) Ovid tells the story of Baucis and Philemon, an aged but poor couple whom Jupiter in his wanderings found to be especially hospitable and pious. Jupiter spared them when all their neighbors were drowned in a flood. How does this story compare with that of Deucalion and Pyrrha? Is it simply a doublet?
5) There is possible historical evidence for a great flood in the Black Sea about 7000 years ago as a result of the melting of Ice Age glaciers. Originally the Black Sea was not connected to the Mediterranean. A rush of ice-melt broke through the Bosporus and caused a catastrophic flood. The evidence has been examined by Columbia geologists William Ryan and Walter Pitman. See the website: http://www.national_geographic.com/blacksea.
6) Deucalion and Pyrrha also had a son named Hellen. Of what people and country is he the ancestor?

Cultural Influences

Art: Filarete, "Deucalion and Pyrrha," relief on bronze door of St. Peter's, Rome (1433–45); Jacopo Tintoretto, "Deucalion and Pyrrha Praying before the Statue of the God," painting (c. 1541); Hendrik Goltzius, four engravings featuring the flood, part of a set illustrating Ovid's *Metamorphoses* (c. 1589); Pablo Picasso, "Deucalion and Pyrrha with One of Their Children," etching, illustration for an edition of Ovid's *Metamorphoses* (1930).

Literature: John Milton compares Deucalion and Pyrrha to Adam and Eve in *Paradise Lost* 2.8–14 (1667), and William Vaughn Moody features Deucalion and Pyrrha in *The Fire-Bringer*, a poetic drama (1904).

Music: operas by Paul-César Gibert (1772), Antonio Calegari (1781), and A. Montfort (1855).

Themis

Chapter Eight

THESEUS AND THE MINOTAUR; ARIADNE

Theseus is the great Athenian hero whose story contains many different episodes, including battling the Amazons, abducting the twelve-year old Helen, offering protection to the aged Oedipus, and descending to the underworld. Some of these myths will be included in later chapters. The episode featured here is the one for which he is most famous: the slaying of the Minotaur. Theseus was the child of Aegeus, king of Athens, and a Peloponnesian princess, Aethra, from Troezen. Some versions claim he was actually the son of Neptune. When Aegeus left Troezen he placed a sword and sandals in a hollow under a massive rock. He told Aethra that, if she had a son, when he came of age he could establish his identity by retrieving the sword. When Theseus removed the sword, he travelled to Athens to claim his place as heir to Aegeus. Instead of taking the easy route by sea, he chose to emulate the hero Hercules (Greek Heracles) and thus to take the hazardous journey by land. On his route he confronted and beat many terrible outlaws and monsters. In Athens Aegeus recognized him by his sword and acknowledged Theseus as his son.

At this time Athens had to pay a dreadful tribute every nine years to Minos, King of Crete. Minos' son had been killed in Athens and, as recompense, Minos demanded that the Athenians send seven youths and seven maidens to Crete to feed the Minotaur, a creature with the body of a man but the head of a bull. The Minotaur was imprisoned in the palace of Knossos in a labyrinth built by the ingenious craftsman Daedalus, also an Athenian. Normally the Athenian children were chosen by lot, but Theseus volunteered to put an end to this dreadful tribute. By a combination of luck and bravery Theseus succeeded in his mission.

The passage below is drawn from many sources but most closely follows Catullus.

SOURCES

Bacchylides, *Dithyrambs* 1 & 2 • Euripides, *Hippolytus* • Sophocles, *Oedipus at Colonus* • Catullus 64. 50–266 • Ovid, *Heroides* 10, *Metamorphoses* 7. 404–52, 8. 172–76 • Plutarch, *Lives,* Theseus

nōlēbat: *was unwilling, did not want*
Crēta, -ae, f. - *Crete, large island in the Mediterranean south of Greece*
mōnstrum, -ī, n. - *monster, beast*
pugnō (1) - *to fight*
ōrō (1) - *to beg, beseech*
perstō, -stāre, -stetī, -stātum - *to stand firm, persist, be resolute*
vēlum -ī, n. - *sail*
niger, -gra, -grum - *dark, black*
candidus, -a, -um - *bright, white*
5 mihi: dative of separation, *from me*
invītus, -a, -um - *unwilling, against one's will*
Athēnās: with names of cities a preposition is not used; understand *ad*
reveniō, -īre, -vēnī, -ventum - *to come back, return*
dēpōnō, -ere, -posuī, -positum - *to lay down, take down, get rid of*
sustollō, -ere - *to lift up, raise*
ventus, -ī, m. - *wind*
advehō, -ere, -vexī, -vectum - in passive, *to be carried, sail to*
lūgeō, -ēre, lūxī, lūctum - *to mourn, lament*
aequus, -a, -um - *even, calm*
10 lītus, -toris, n. - *shore*
praesertim (adv.) - *especially*
hērōs, hērōis, m. - *hero*
cōnspiciō, -ere, -spexī, -spectum - *to spot, catch sight of*
statim (adv.) - *immediately*
interficiō, -ere, -fēcī, -fectum - *to kill*
petō, -ere, -īvī, -ītum - *to seek*

Grammar and Comprehension Questions

1) What case is *nāvis*?
2) What case is *fīliō* and why?
3) What person, number, and tense is *advehēbantur*?

Theseus and the Minotaur; Ariadne 57

Rēx Aegeus nōlēbat fīlium suum ad Crētam nāvigāre et mōnstrum pugnāre. Aegeus ōrābat Thēseum remanēre, sed fortis Thēseus perstābat. Vēla **nāvis** erant nigra, quod illa nāvis puerōs puellāsque ad mortem portābat. Aegeus **fīliō** candida vēla dedit. Dīxit: "Fortūna et virtūs tua tē mihi invītō ēripiunt. Sī salvus Athēnās reveniēs, nigra   5
vēla dēpōne et candida vēla sustolle. Sīc cognoscam tē esse salvum."

Thēseus et miserī puerī puellaeque vēla ventō dedērunt et mox ad Crētam **advehēbantur**. Omnēs lūgēbant timēbantque. Sōlus Thēseus aequum animum tenēbat. Thēseus aut mortem aut laudem petēbat. In lītore Ariadna, fīlia rēgis Crētae, nāvem et praesertim bellum   10
hērōem cōnspexit. Statim magnus amor Thēseī Ariadnam cēpit.

Discussion Questions

1) Why did the ship sail from Athens with black sails? What does this symbolize?
2) What would we call the type of love Ariadne instantly feels for Theseus? Can you find other instances of such love in mythology? What causes such love?

Greek ship with black sails

dēcernō, -ere, -crēvī, crētum - *to decide, settle, decree*
Athēnaeus, -ī, m. - *Athenian*
carcer, -ceris, m. - *jail, prison*
nox, noctis, f. - *night*
occultē (adv.) - *secretly*
susurrō (1) - *to whisper*
15   fīlum, -ī, n. - *thread, string*
gladius, -iī, m. - *sword*
effugiō, -ere, -fūgī - *to escape, flee*
intrō (1) - *to walk into, enter*
dēdūcō, -ere, -dūxī, -ductum - *to draw out*
postquam (conj.) - *after*
extrā (adv.) - *outside*
rēgō, -ere, rēxī, rēctum - *to rule, guide, direct*
prex, precis, f. - *prayer*
abdūcō, -ere, dūxī, -ductum - *to lead away, take away*
prope (prep. + acc.) - *near*
20
stupeō, -ēre, -uī - *to be astounded, stunned*
laetus, -a, -um - *happy, joyful*
nūbō, -ere, nūpsī, nūptum (+ dat.) - *to marry*

prōmittō, -ere, -mīsī, -missum - *to promise*
praeter (prep. + acc.) - *except*
prehendō, -dere, -dī, -sum - *to take hold of, grasp*
flexus, -ūs, m. - *bending, winding, turning*
25   procul (adv.) - *far, at a distance*
postrēmō (adv.) - *finally*
angulus, -ī, m. - *corner, angle*
vertō, -ere, vertī, versum - *to turn, change*
ecce (interjection) - *behold! look!*
horrendē (adv.) - *terribly, awfully*
fremō, -ere, -uī, -itum - *to snort, roar*
oppugnō (1) - *to attack*
medius, -a, -um - *middle; the middle of*
pectus, -toris, n. - *chest, heart*
pellō, -ere, pepulī, pulsum - *to strike, push, drive*
nēquīquam (adv.) - *in vain, uselessly*
iactō (1) - *to toss, throw*
gemō, -ere, -uī, -itum - *to groan*
sanguis, -guinis, m. - *blood*
relinquō, -ere, -līquī, -lictum - *to leave behind*

Grammar and Comprehension Questions

1) Identify the person, number, tense, and voice of *ductī sunt*.
2) Pronounce the word *susurrāvit*. What effect is created? What do you call the effect?
3) What tense is *interfēceris*?
4) What did Theseus promise Ariadne?
5) How does Theseus react differently than his fellow Athenians?
6) To what does *id* refer?
7) What case, number, and gender is *cornua*?

Puella igitur timēbat quod Thēseus saevum mōnstrum interficere cupiēbat. Ariadna dēcrēvit hērōem iuvāre. Athēnaeī ad carcerem **ductī sunt.** Nocte Ariadna ad Thēseum occultē vēnit et **susurrāvit**: "Ego, Ariadna, fīlia rēgis, tē amō et iuvāre cupiō. Hoc fīlum et hunc 15
gladium cape. Inveniēs Mīnōtaurum in magnō labyrinthō ē quō difficile est effugere. Intrā in labyrinthum et fīlum post tē dēdūce. Postquam Mīnōtaurum **interfēceris**, hoc fīlum ē labyrinthō tē reget. Ūnam precem orō. Abdūce mē tēcum Athēnās. Prope nāvem tē exspectābō." 20
Thēseus stupēbat sed laetus dōna cēpit. Etiam Ariadnae nūbere prōmīsit, sī salvus mōnstrum vīcit. Omnēs Athēnaeī in labyrinthum actī sunt. Terror omnēs praeter Thēseum habēbat. Thēseus gladium prehendit et in obscūrum labyrinthum intrāvit. Multōs flexūs, multās viās invēnit. Etiam mōnstrum procul audiēbat, sed non 25
poterat **id** invenīre. Postrēmō in angulum vertit et—ecce! Mīnōtaurus aderat et horrendē fremēbat. Statim Thēseus gladiō oppugnāvit et medium pectus Mīnōtaurī pepulīt. Nēquīquam Mīnōtaurus **cornua** iactabat. Mōnstrum gemuit et multō sanguine vītam relīquit.

Discussion Questions

1) In helping Theseus, whom is Ariadne betraying?
2) The place of Minos at Knossos has been excavated. Examine the floor plan. Do you see a connection between this and the story above?
3) Study the myth of the Minotaur's origin. Also, study the use of bulls in Cretan art. What sport involves them?
4) A European folktale uses a similar device to Theseus' thread to retrace steps. What story is it? Who are the characters?
5) Labyrinths or mazes have been featured in many settings. There is a famous maze at Hampton Court in London, England. For a more modern image see the film *The Shining* (1980) based upon the Stephen King novel. *The Simpsons'* episode *The Shinning* (1986) parodied the film. Also see the movie *Labyrinth* with Jim Henson's Muppets (1986). What other examples of labyrinths and mazes can you find?

Cultural Influences

To list all the art, literature, and music inspired by Theseus and the Minotaur would require many pages. There are operas in abundance including by Handel (1713); ballets by Balanchine (1962) and Ashton (1964); and plays, as well as innumberable art works. The following is a very modest selection:

Historical Novels: by Mary Renault *The King Must Die* (1958) and *The Bull from the Sea* (1962).

Painting: Sandro Botticelli, Minotaur drawing illustrating Dante's *Inferno* 12 (1480s–90s); William Blake, watercolor, "The Minotaur" (1824–27); George Frederick Watts, painting "The Minotaur" (1885). Pablo Picasso created more than a dozen illustrations of the Minotaur from 1928–52. The Minotaur became one of his favorite themes.

Sculpture: Filarete, "Theseus and the Minotaur," a relief on the bronze door of St. Peter's, Rome (1433–45); Antonio Canova, marble "Theseus and the Minotaur" (1781–83); Auguste Rodin, painted plaster "The Minotaur" (1886); Leonard Baskin, bronzes "The Minotaur" and "Theseus" (1969); Paul Wunderlich, metal "Minotaur" (1977).

Theseus slays the Minotaur

Theseus and the Minotaur

Chapter Nine

THE FATES OF ARIADNE AND AEGEUS

This reading continues the Theseus episode. After slaying the Minotaur he leaves Crete, accompanied by Ariadne. In Athens Aegeus anxiously awaits his return. Again the phraseology and story line rely primarily on the Catullan version in his poem 64.

fīlum, -ī, n. - *thread, string*
postquam (conj.) - *after*
interficiō, -ere, -fēcī, -fectum - *to kill*
vestīgium -iī, n. - *footstep, track*
tenuis, -e - *delicate, fine, slender*
iānua, -ae, f. - *door, gate*
cēterī, -ae, -a - *other*
effugiō, -ere, -fūgī - *to escape, flee*
occultē (adv.) - *secretly*
5 celeritās, -tātis, f. - *speed, swiftness*
vēlum -ī, n. - *sail*
ventus, -ī, m. - *wind*
proximus, -a, -um - *next*
Naxon: Greek accusative singular, *Naxos*, an island between Crete and mainland Greece
advehō, -ere, vexī, -vectum - in passive, *to be carried, sail to*
torus, -ī, m. - *marriage bed*
coniungō, -ere, -iūnxī, -iūnctum - *to join together, unite*
somnus, -ī, m. - *sleep*
excitō (1) - *to rouse, wake*
statim (adv.) - *immediately*
prōmissum, -ī, n. - *promise*
10 dēsertus, -a, -um - *deserted, abandoned*

unda, -ae, f. - *wave*
fluctuō (1) - *to be tossed about, to seethe*
clāmō (1) - *to shout, cry aloud*
crūdēlis, -e - *cruel*
flectō, -ere, flexī, flexum - *to bend, turn, change, alter*
clēmentia, -ae, f. - *mercy, kindness, clemency*
tibi: dative of possession, *for you; do you have?*
blandus, -a, -um - *charming, pleasing, enticing*
vōx, vōcis, f. - *voice, word*
spērō (1) - *to hope for, hope*
cōnūbium, -iī, n. - *marriage*
laetus, -a, -um - *joyful, happy*
15 perfidus, -a, -um - *faithless, treacherous, false, deceitful*
adventus, -ūs, m. - *arrival*
dolor, -lōris, m. - *grief, sorrow*
portus, -ūs, m. - *harbor*
adveniō, -īre, -vēnī, -ventum - *to come (to), arrive*
scopulus, -ī, m. - *high rock, crag, cliff*
dēspiciō, -ere, -spexī, -spectum - *to look down*

Grammar and Comprehension Questions

1) Where did Ariadne wait for Theseus?
2) What does *magnā* modify?
3) How does Ariadne interpret the night she spent with Jason *in torō*?
4) What does the *-ne* in *nūllane* indicate?
5) To what promises does Ariadne refer?
6) What effect does the juxtaposition of *ego* and *tē* create?
7) What case and number is *perfide*?

The Fates of Ariadne and Aegeus

Postquam Thēseus mōnstrum interfēcit, ē labyrinthō vestīgia tenuī
fīlō rēxit et iterum ad iānuam labyrinthī vēnit, ubi cēterī Athēnaeī
remanēbant. Omnēs gaudēbant et Thēseum laudābant. Nocte ad
nāvem effūgērunt, ubi Ariadna occultē manēbat. **Magnā** cum
celeritāte vēla ventīs dedērunt. Proximō diē ad īnsulam Naxon[1] 5
advectī sunt. Ibi noctem agēbant et Thēseus Ariadnaque **in torō**
coniunxērunt.

Prīmō diē Thēseus Athēnaeōs ē somnō excitāvit et statim eōs
vēla ventīs dare iūssit. Thēseus nāvigāvit et prōmissa ventīs relīquit.
Sed Ariadna mox sē ē somnō excitāvit et sē dēsertam invēnit. Misera 10
ē lītore celerem nāvem vīdit. Ariadna magnīs cūrārum undīs fluctuat.
Clāmat Thēseum: "**Nūllane** rēs potuit crūdēlem mentem flectere?
Nūlla clēmentia tibi fuit? Nōn haec prōmissa mihi blandā vōce
dedistī. Nōn haec mē mīseram spērāre iubēbās, sed cōnūbia laeta.
Ego tē ē magnō perīculō, etiam ē morte ēripuī. Nunc tū, **perfide**, 15
mē in dēsertō lītore relinquis. Sī deī mē audiunt, adventus tuus
magnum dolōrem faciet."

Nunc nāvis ad portum adveniēbat. Aegeus dē summō scopulō
diū dēspiciēbat.

Discussion Questions

1) Why do you think Theseus left Ariadne? Did he simply forget her? Or was he heartless? Or is there another explanation?
2) What does Ariadne pray will happen to Theseus?
3) Compare the figure of Ariadne deserted by Theseus with Dido when Aeneas leaves Carthage. Did Vergil use the Ariadne story as a model?

---

[1] Catullus names the island Dia as the landing place. It is a very small island just off the northern coast of Crete. Most mythological sources, however, say that they landed on Naxos, a much larger island further to the northeast, which was famous for wine. In the context of the end of the story, Naxos makes better sense as the setting.

20 **mandātum, -ī, n.** - *order, command, instruction*
prius (adv.) - *before*
fīdus, -a, -um - *faithful, trustworthy, reliable*
dēdiscō, -ere, -dicī - *to forget*
etiamnunc (adv.) - *still*
niger, -gra, -grum - *dark, black*
mortuus, -a, -um - *dead*
crēdō, -ere, -didī, -ditum - *to believe, trust*
dēspērō (1) - *to despair*
25 **certē** (adv.) - *certainly, surely*
fera, -ae, f. - *wild animal*
vorō (1) - *to eat, devour*

famēs, -is, f. - *hunger*
pereō, -īre, -iī, -itum - *to perish, die*
sonitus, -ūs, m. - *sound*
satyrus, -ī, m. - *satyr, a demi-god of wild places; half-man, half-goat*
Baccha, -ae, f. - *Bacchante (female devotee of Bacchus)*
volitō (1) - *to move quickly to and fro, roam about*
pallēscō, -ere, -uī - *to grow pale*
pulchritūdō, -dinis, f. - *beauty*
30 **corōna, -ae, f.** - *crown*
boreālis, -e - *northern*

Grammar and Comprehension Questions

1) What gender, number, and case is *quae*? What is its antecedent?
2) What did Aegeus do when he saw the black sails?
3) What tense and person is *faciam*?
4) What does Ariadne think will happen to her on the deserted island?
5) What case and number is *eī*? To whom does it refer?

Bacchus

Thēseus autem omnia mandāta patris, **quae** prius fīdā mente 20
tenēbat, dēdicit. Vēla etiamnunc nigra erant. Aegeus nigra vēla
vīdit et statim dē scopulō in mare sē iēcit. Nam crēdidit Thēseum,
filium suum, esse mortuum.

Sed Ariadna, etiamnunc in dēsertō lītore, dēspērābat et multās
cūrās in mente volvēbat. "Quid **faciam**? Certē aut ferae mē vorābunt 25
aut fame perībō." Ariadna igitur omnem sonitum timēbat. At in aliā
parte īnsulae deus Bacchus cum satyrīs et Bacchīs volitābat. Satyrī
Bacchaeque multum novum sonitum fēcerunt. Ariadna adventum
eōrum audīvit et timōre pallēscēbat. Bacchus autem pulchritūdinem
eius vīdit et cupiēbat eam esse uxōrem suam. Ariadna igitur in 30
Olympō cum deīs vīvit. Bacchus dōnum matrimōniī **eī** dedit,
corōnam borealem, quae in caelō vidēre potes.[2]

Discussion Questions

1) What was strange about the sound the satyrs and Bacchantes made? What did Ariadne hear? What other name exists for the Bacchantes?
2) Why did Theseus forget his father's instructions?
3) Why is the sea near Athens called Aegean?
4) The Corona Borealis is a constellation. Where is it in the sky? What does it look like?

---

[2] In other versions of the myth the crown was a gift from Theseus, which Dionysus then tossed into the sky. Homer's *Odyssey* 11.321–25 reports that the goddess Artemis, at Dionysus' (Bacchus) order, killed Ariadne on the island of Dia before Theseus could enjoy their love. This brief account hints at a very different version from the story that has come down to us.

Cultural Influences

Once again, the wealth of material generated by the myth of Ariadne is enormous. The following is a brief representative selection.

Art: Ariadne abandoned was one of the most popular themes of painters, particularly in the seventeenth century. Many painters created multiple versions. Henri Fanton-Latour (1836–1904) alone created 11 separate paintings on the theme. A brief historical survey: Titian, "Bacchus and Ariadne" (1520–23) and "Ariadne on Naxos" (1576); Tintoretto, "The Marriage of Bacchus and Ariadne in the Presence of Venus" (1577–78) and "Venus, Bacchus and Ariadne" (1580s); Jan Brueghel the Elder, "The Marriage Feast of Bacchus" (1606–07); "Bacchus and Ariadne" by Nicolas Poussin (1620s) and Peter Paul Rubens (1636–38); Claude Lorrain, "Coast View of Naxos with Ariadne and Bacchus" (1656); Eustace LeSueur, "Bacchus and Ariadne" (1640); Jacob Jordaens, "Discovery of Ariadne by Bacchus" (late 1640s); John Vanderlyn, "Ariadne asleep on Naxos" (1812); George Frederic Watts, "Ariadne on Naxos" (1875 and 1894). For sculpture, see Donatello, marble relief (1466) and Auguste Rodin, "Ariadne," marble (1889).

Literature: Geoffrey Chaucer, "The Legend of Ariadne," poem in *The Legende of Goode Women* (1385–86); Elizabeth Barrett Browning "How Bacchus Finds Ariadne Sleeping" and "How Bacchus Comforts Ariadne," two poems in *Last Poems* (1845); Robert Graves, "Theseus and Ariadne," poem (1945).

Music: Ariadne has inspired literally dozens of operas (e.g., Monteverdi, 1608; Handel, 1734; Haydn, 1790). The best known is by Richard Strauss, *Ariadne auf Naxos* (1912). There are also numerous ballets dating from 1459 (Bergonzio di Botta) to the twentieth century (Duncan, Massine, Graham, Ailey, Balanchine).

Bacchus onboard

Chapter Ten

Daedalus and Icarus: Man-Powered Flight

Daedalus was an ingenious Athenian craftsman who designed and built the Cretan labyrinth for Minos. In fact, his name in Greek means "cunning worker" and the Latin adjective *daedalus, -a, -um* means "skillful." Minos imprisoned Daedalus and his son Icarus in Crete, either to prevent disclosure of the secret plan of the labyrinth, or because Daedalus had assisted Ariadne in her rescue of Theseus. Since there was no exit by land or water, Daedalus turned to the only alternative: the sky. The following reading is modeled closely on the Ovidian version.

Sources

Vergil, *Aeneid* 6. 14–33 • Horace, *Odes* 4.2. 1–4 • Ovid, *Metatmorphoses* 8. 155–232

exsilium -iī, n. - *exile, banishment*
Mīnōs, -ōis, m. - *Minos, king of Crete*
claudō, -ere, clausī, clausum - *to shut, close*
pateō, -ēre, -uī - *to lie open, be open, be accessible*
praebeō, -ēre, -uī, -itum - *to offer, provide*
ignōtus, -a, -um - *unknown, obscure*
dīmittō, -ere, -mīsī, -missum - *to send forth, direct*
ōrdō, -dinis, m. - *rank, order*
penna, -ae, f. - *feather*
pōnō, -ere, posuī, positum - *to place, put, set*
linum, -ī, n. - *thread, string*
cēra, -ae, f. - *wax*
5 **alligō (1)** - *to tie up, bind*
curāmen, -minis, n. - *arc, curved form*
flectō, -ere, flexī, flexum - *to bend, form*
prope (prep. + acc.) - *near*
ignārus, -a, -um (+ gen.) - *not knowing, ignorant (of)*
īnstrūmentum, -ī, n. - *device, equipment, tool*
gaudeō, -ēre, gāvīsus sum - *to rejoice, be glad*
temptō (1) - *to try, test*
geminus, -a, -um - *twin*

āla, -ae, f. - *wing*
lībrō (1) - *to balance, hang suspended*
āēr, āeris, m. - *air*
pendeō, -ēre, pependī - *to hang suspended, hang*
īnferior: nominative singular masculine adjective, *lower*
volō (1) - *to fly*
gravō (1) - *to make heavy, weigh down*
altior: nominative singular masculine adjective, *higher*
10 **dissolvō, -ere, -solvī, -solūtum** - *to loosen, break up, dissolve*
lacrimō (1) - *to weep, shed tears*
umerus, -ī, m. - *shoulder, upper arm*
accommodō (1) - *to fit, put on*
tremō, -ere, -uī - *to tremble*
ōsculum, -ī, n. - *kiss*
levō (1) - *to raise, lift up*
sequī: present infinitive, *to follow*
ambō, ambae, ambō - *both*
pastor, -tōris, m. - *shepherd*
arātor, -tōris, m. - *ploughman*
stupeō, -ēre, -uī - *to be astounded, stunned*
15 **crēdō, -ere, -didī, -ditum** - *to believe, trust*
audāx, -ācis - *daring, bold*
volātus, -ūs, m. - *flight*

Grammar and Comprehension Questions

1) Where is Daedalus' *patria*?
2) Who is the subject of *dīmīsit*?
3) From what materials does Daedalus fashion wings?
4) What tense are *stābat* and *gaudēbat*? What time does this tense emphasize?
5) Does Icarus feel any fear about the attempt to fly? What are Daedalus' emotions?
6) What case is *Īcare*?
7) What tense is *dissolvet*?
8) What do the spectators believe that Daedalus and Icarus are?

Daedalus longum exsilium in Crētā ōdit et **patriam** vidēre cupiēbat.
Sibi dīxit: "Mīnōs terrās et mare claudit. Caelum autem patet. Mīnōs
caelum nōn regit. Caelum viam praebēbit." Tum animum in ignōtās
artēs **dīmīsit**. Nam in ōrdine pennās posuit. Tum eās līnō et cērā
alligāvit et in curvāmen flexit. Puer Īcarus prope patrem **stābat** et, 5
ignārus perīculōrum, in novō īnstrūmentō **gaudēbat**. Pater
īnstrūmentum temptāvit—ipse corpus in geminīs ālīs lībrāvit et in
āere pependit! Tum etiam fīlium docuit et monēbat. "**Īcare**, in mediā
viā curre. Moneō: sī īnferior volābis, mare pennās gravābit; sī altior
volābis, sōl cēram **dissolvet**. Volā ubi tē dūcō." 10
    Ut Daedalus dīcēbat, lacrimābat et ālās umerīs fīliī accomodābat.
Manūs tremēbant. Tum ōscula fīliō dedit. Postrēmō ālīs sē in āerem
levāvit et iūssit Īcarum sequī. Ambō ālās movēbant et per āerem
volābant. Pastor et arātor eōs vīdērunt et stupuērunt, quod
crēdidērunt eōs esse deōs. Iam Crētam et multās īnsulās relīquērunt. 15
Īcarus autem nimis in audacī volātū gaudēre coepit.

Discussion Question

1) *Pastor* in Latin means "shepherd." What is the English meaning? Do you see a connection between the two meanings?
2) In mythology who else flies? How?
3) Examine the early history of flight. What was the first true human flight? In what device?

dēserō, -ere, -uī, -ertum - *to desert, abandon, leave*
altiōrem: accusative singular feminine adjective, *higher*
agō, -ere, ēgī, actum - *to drive, take*
molliō, -īre, -īvī, -ītum - *to soften*
nūdus, -a, -um - *bare*

20 **clāmō** (1) - *to call, shout, cry aloud*
timidus, -a, -um - *fearful*
dēvoveō, -ēre, -ōvī, -ōtum - *to curse*
repetō, -ere, -īvī, -ītum - *to seek again*
sepulchrum, -ī, n. - *tomb*

Grammar and Comprehension Questions

1) Why did the wings fall apart?
2) What do you call the clause *quae pennās habēbat*?
3) What case is *ōs* and what is its function?
4) What did Daedalus see floating on the sea?
5) What case is *corpus*?

Brueghel woodcut, *The Fall of Icarus*

Nunc Icarus ducem dēseruit et altiōrem viam ēgit. Sed sōl cēram, **quae pennās habēbat**, mollīvit. Iam ille nūdōs umerōs movēbat; sine pennīs āerem nōn tenēbat. Clāmāvit "pater," sed mare **ōs** clausit. Timidus pater, nec iam pater, "Īcare," dīxit, "ubi es?" Pennās in marī vīdit dēvōvitque artēs suās. Miser Daedalus terram repetīvit. **Corpus** in sepulchrō posuit. Mare ubi Icarus cecidit ā nōmine Īcarī dictum est. 20

Discussion Questions

1) Find the Icarian Sea. How near is it to Crete? How far off course did Icarus fly?
2) Man-powered (versus machine-powered) flight has always been a human dream. What inventors attempted it? A man-powered flight by "Daedalus 88" of 199 kilometers from Crete to Santorini was completed in 1988. It took three hours and fifty-four minutes. How was it achieved? Who did it? See the website www.dfrc.nasa.gov/gallery/photo/Daedalus/. You can also research the machine called the Gossamer Albatross.

Cretan labyrinth

Cultural Influences

Again extremely numerous, perhaps because of artistic fascination with the artist Daedalus. The following gives a sense of the broad range of influence.

Art: Filarete, reliefs on the bronze door of St. Peter's, Rome (1433–45); Pieter Brueghel, "Landscape with the fall of Icarus," painting (c. 1558); Peter Paul Rubens, "The Fall of Icarus," painting (1636–38); Charles-Paul Landon, "Daedalus and Icarus," painting (1799); Henri Matisse, "Falling Icarus," lithograph (1947); "The Fall of Icarus" by Pablo Picasso (mural in UNESCO building, Paris, 1957); paintings by Salvador Dali (1963) and Marc Chagall (1974). There are also statues by Canova (1777), Rodin (1880–02), and numerous twentieth century sculptors (Martini, Paolozzi, Bertoni, Hunt, Mascherini, Andreou, Mooy, Ayrton, Manship, Baskin, and Lekberg).

Literature: Francis Bacon, "Daedalus, sive Mechanicus" and "Scylla, et Icarus, sive viamedia," Chapters 19 & 27 of *De sapientia veterum* (1609). James Joyce names his hero Stephen Dedalus in both *Portrait of the Artist as a Young Man* (1916) and his epic *Ulysses* (1922). The theme of Daedalus and Icarus is woven throughout both works.

Music: There are operas dating from 1817 (Volkert) to 1981 (Forman). Ballets date from 1818 (Vigano) to 1935 (Serge Lifar, for which Picasso created the backcloth design). Other ballets are by King, Vasiliev, Milloss, Belsky, Arpino, Ormiston, and even an ice ballet by Butler (1977).

Mythical Variations

In other versions Daedalus landed on Sicily, to the west of Crete. In Vergil's version in *Aeneid* 6 Daedalus landed in Italy at Cumae near Naples. He then dedicated his wings to Apollo and commemorated his unique trip by creating bronze doors that detailed the story of Minos, the Minotaur, and the labyrinth. His sorrow for Icarus prevented him from including his fall.

Daedalus Watches Icarus' Fall

Chapter Eleven

The History of Bacchus: Semele and Pentheus

The readings in the next few chapters turn from the Athenian mythical cycle to the Theban cycle.

The god Bacchus or Liber (in Greek, Dionysus) is unusual in that he is one of the youngest gods and yet one of the most prominent in Greek legend and daily life. As the god of wine he was very frequently depicted on drinking vessels of all sorts. These depictions often include his attendant satyrs and women devotees, called Bacchantes or Maenads. Bacchus usually holds a cup and is surrounded by vines and ivy. Bacchus, as the god of revelry and ecstasy, is often contrasted with Apollo, who represents rationality and order.

The reading here concerns, first, Bacchus' extraordinary birth in Thebes and then his controversial arrival as a young adult god in the city of his birth. Bacchus is the son of Jupiter and a mortal woman, Semele, daughter of the Theban king Cadmus. The reading is modeled on the Ovidian version.

Sources

Hesiod, *Theogony* 940–42 • Pindar, *Olympian Odes* 2.21–27 • Euripides, *Bacchae* • Ovid, *Metamorphoses* 3. 259–315 (Semele), 511–733 (Pentheus)

Semelē, -ēs, f. - *Semele*, Theban princess
gravidus, -a, -um - *pregnant*
doleō, -ēre, -uī, -itum - *to grieve*
praesertim (adv.) - *especially*
aemula, -ae, f. - *rival*
perdō, -ere, perdidī, perditum - *to destroy*
statuō, -ere, -uī, -ūtum - *to decide*
domum: understand *ad: to the home, house*
anus, -ūs, f. - *old woman*
serva, -ae, f. - *female servant*
suscipiō, -ere, -cēpī, -ceptum - *to take on, assume*
anīlis, -e - *of an old woman*
amātor, -tōris, m. - *lover*
5 **dēcipiō, -ere, -cēpī, -ceptum** - *to deceive*
pignus, -neris, n. - *guarantee, proof*
veniat: subjunctive mood (see Wheelock, Ch. 28), *let him come*
īnsigne, -is, n. - *personal decoration or mark of honor; visible token, attribute*
mūnus, -neris, n. - *gift*
rogāvit: the verb takes a double accusative, of the person asked and the thing asked for
ēligō, -ligere, -lēgī, -lectum - *to choose, select*

quisquis, quisquid - *whoever, whatever*
iūrō (1) + acc. of thing sworn by - *to swear by*
Stygius, -a, -um - *Stygian*; the underworld river Styx by which the gods swore unbreakable oaths
10 **gemō, -ere, -uī, -itum** - *to groan*
prex, precis, f. - *prayer*
remittō, -ere, -mīsī, -missum - *to take back, let go*
negō (1) - *to deny, refuse*
ergō (adv.) - *therefore*
tollō, -ere, sustulī, sublātum - *to raise, lift up*
addō, -ere, -didī, -ditum - *to add*
fulgur, -uris, n. - *flash of lightning*
tonitrus, -ūs, m. - *thunder*
intrō (1) - *to walk into, enter*
tumultus, -ūs, m. - *uprising, disturbance, tumult*
ardeō, -ēre, arsī - *to catch fire, burn, be burnt to death*
15 **nōndum** (adv.) - *not yet*
alvus, -ī, f. - *womb, belly*
dignus, -a, -um - *worthy*
femur, -moris, n. - *thigh*
īnsuō, -ere, -uī, -ūtum - *to sew up (in)*
reliquus, -a, -um - *remaining*
impleō, -ēre, -lēvī, -lētum - *to fill up, complete*

Grammar and Comprehension Questions

1) Whom did Juno imitate?
2) What gender, number, and case is *multī*? What is it understood to modify?
3) What is meant by *omnibus cum īnsignibus*? How would Jupiter appear? What is dangerous?
4) What gender, number, and case is *illa*? To whom does it refer?
5) What does *mixta* modify?
6) What do we call the type of birth Dionysus experienced?
7) Where did Dionysus complete his growth before birth?

Semelē erat gravida ē Iove. Iūnō autem dolēbat quod Iuppiter aliam fēminam, praesertim mortālem, amābat. Dea igitur aemulam suam perdere statuit. Iūnō domum Semelēs vēnit et formam anūs, servae Semelēs suscēpit. Serva anīlī vōce dīxit: "Amātor tuus nōmen 'Iuppiter' suscipit, sed **multī** nōmine deōrum fēminās dēcēpērunt. 5
Quārē rogā pignus. Veniat ad tē omnibus cum īnsignibus." Semelē anuī crēdidit. Mox igitur Semelē Iovem mūnus rogāvit. Deus respondit "Ēlige. Tibi dabō quidquid cupis. Iūrō flūmen Stygium." Semelē tum rogāvit: "Venī ad mē omnibus cum **insignibus**, ut ad Iūnōnem venīs." Iuppiter gemuit, nam nec **illa** precem remittere nec 10
ipse negāre poterat. Ergō miser deus in caelum ascendit et fulmen, quō mortālēs terret, tollit. Addidit nūbēs et fulgura ventīs **mixta** et tonitrum. Tum dēscendit et domum Semelēs intrāvit. Sed corpus mortāle aetherium tumultum tolerāre nōn poterat et arsit. Sed Iuppiter īnfantem Bacchum, nōndum perfectum, ex alvō mātris 15
ēripuit et (sī crēdere dignum est) in femorī suō īnsuit. Ibi Bacchus reliquum tempus implēvit.

Discussion Questions

1) What would happen to a god who broke his oath by the Styx?
2) We talk of lightning and thunder. In Latin Jupiter wields *tonitrus*, *fulgur*, and *fulmen*. What are they? How does this differ from our interpretation?

nātus est: *was born*
nympha, -ae, f. - *nymph,* semi-divine female spirit of nature
Nȳsa, -ae, f. - *Nysa,* legendary mountain, usually located in India, where Bacchus was born
clam (adv.) - *secretly, under cover*
20 iuvenis, -is, m. - *young man, a youth*
vīnum, -ī, n. - *wine*
praebeō, -ēre, -uī, -itum - *to offer, provide*
Thēbae, -ārum, f. pl. - *Thebes,* city in Greece
Thēbās: with cities the preposition *ad* may be omitted.
Thēbānus, -a, -um - *Theban*
cōnsōbrīnus, -ī, m. - *maternal cousin.* Pentheus is the son of Agave, who is Semele's sister.
spernō, -ere, sprēvī, sprētum - *to scorn, despise, spurn*
Tīrēsiās, -ae, m. - *Tiresias,* legendary blind prophet of Thebes
vātēs, -is, m. - *prophet, seer*
25 spargō, -ere, sparsī, sparsum - *to scatter, spread, strew*
foedō (1) - *to soil, stain, foul, defile, pollute*
clāmor, -mōris, m. - *shout, cry*
fremō, -ere, -uī, -itum - *to resound, roar*
sacra, -ōrum, n. pl. - *sacred rites*

30 castīgō (1) - *to chastise, criticize*
sacerdōs, -dōtis, m. - *priest*
carcer, -ceris, m. - *jail, prison*
sponte: ablative feminine singular, *will, accord*
solvō, -ere, -uī, -ūtum - *to loosen, undo, untie*
aperiō, -īre, -uī, -tum - *to open*
Cithaerōn, -rōnis, m. - *Mount Cithaeron,* near Thebes, associated with Bacchus
euhoe (interjection) - the cry of the Bacchantes
clāmō (1) - *to call, shout, cry aloud*
profānus, -a, -um - *uninitiated, profane, impious*
Agāvē, -ēs, f. - *Agave,* mother of Pentheus, sister of Semele
thyrsus, - ī, m. - *thyrsus,* a wand or staff tipped with a pine-cone and wound with ivy, symbol of Bacchus carried by the Bacchantes
trānsfīgō, -ere, -fīxī, -fīxum - *to pierce through, transfix*
aper, aprī, m. - *wild boar*
35 furiōsus, -a, -um - *frenzied, mad, raving*
lacerō (1) - *to tear, rend, mangle*
umerus, -ī, m. - *shoulder, upper arm*
āvellō, -ere, -vellī, -volsum - *to tear or wrench away*
potestās, -tātis, f. - *power*

Grammar and Comprehension Questions

1) Can you see the derivation of Dionysus' name? (Jupiter is *Zeus, Dios* in Greek).
2) How does Pentheus offend Dionysus?
3) What verb form is *solūta sunt* and what does *solūta* modify?
4) To whom does *suam* refer?
5) Did the words of Tiresias come true?

Postquam Bacchus nātus est, Iuppiter eum nymphīs in Nȳsā dedit.
Nymphae parvum deum clam alēbant.
   Nunc deus est iuvenis. Hominēs eum adōrant, quod vīnum   20
praebet. Bacchus multīs cum satyrīs Bacchīsque Thēbās vēnit.
Thēbānus populus quoque deum adorābant, sed Pentheus, rēx
Thēbārum et cōnsōbrīnus Bacchī, deum spernēbat. Tīresiās, caecus
vātēs, rēgem monuit: "Nisi hunc deum adōrās, mox deus ipse in mille
locōs tē sparget et sanguine tuō silvās mātremque tuam sorōrēsque   25
mātris foedābis." Pentheus autem vātem neglēxit.
   Bacchus adest et agrī clāmōribus fremunt. Turba virōrum
fēminārumque ad sacra ruit. At Pentheus cīvēs castīgat atque
sacerdōtem deī in vincula et carcerem iacit. Mox vincula dē manibus
sponte suā **solūta sunt** et portae carceris apertae sunt. Laetus   30
sacerdōs ad montēs et Bacchās currit. Pentheus ipse ad Cithaerōnem
ruit, ubi Bacchae "euhoe" clāmābant. Īrātus rēx sacra profānīs oculīs
clam vidēbat. Tum māter Agāvē prīma fīlium vīdit et thyrsō eum
trānsfīxit. Māter clāmāvit: "Ō sorōrēs, currite. Illum aprum, quī in
nostrīs agrīs errat, necāre necesse est. Iuvāte mē!" Omnēs furiōsae   35
in Pentheum ruunt et lacerant. Miser Pentheus clāmat: "Ecce, māter!
Fīlius tuus sum." Sed Agāvē īnsāna caput eius ab umerīs āvellit, in
manibus tenet, et clāmat: "Hoc est victōria nostra!" Sīc deus
potestātem **suam** dēmonstrāvit.

Discussion Questions

   1) Why is the god Dionysus associated with the East?
   2) The god Bacchus is the son of a mortal woman. Jupiter had many other
      sons by mortal women. Who are they? Are they gods as well?
   3) In the reading above there are many words which have direct English
      derivatives. For instance, find the English words that derive from
      īnsignibus, sacra, solūta, lacerō. What others can you find?

Cultural Influences

Art: paintings by Jacopo Tintoretto, "Semele Burned to Ashes" (c. 1541) and "Jupiter and Semele" (several versions, 1541ff.); Peter Paul Rubens (1636–38); Gustave Moreau (1894–95); an etching by Pablo Picasso (1930).

Ballet: on the Bacchantes by Martha Graham: *Three Choric Dances for an Antique Greek Tragedy* (1933); also Yorgos Sicilianos, *Bacchantes (1959–60).*

Literature: Francis Bacon, "Actaeon et Pentheus, sive Curiosus" and "Dionysus, sive Cupiditas," in *De sapientia veterum* (1609); poems by Algernon Swinburne, "Tiresias" (1871); H. D., "Chorus from *The Bacchae*" (1931); George Seferis, "Pentheus" (1955).

Music: choral works on Semele by many composers including Telemann (1716), Handel (1744), and Paul Dukas (1889). Operas on Pentheus and the Bacchae by several composers from Charles-Hubert Gervais in 1705 to Chester Kallmann in 1966 (with lyrics by W. H. Auden). Karol Szymanowski composed *Agave* a cantata for alto, female chorus, and orchestra in 1917.

Mythical Variations

In Euripides' tragedy *Bacchae,* Agave mistakes her son for a young lion rather than a boar. The myth of the hunter Actaeon is also relevant here. Actaeon was Pentheus' cousin, the son of Autonoe, another sister of Agave and Semele. He fatally offended the goddess Artemis, who in vengeance turned him into a deer whom his own hunting dogs then devoured.

— The History of Bacchus: Semele and Pentheus — 83

Juno's Vengeance against Semele

Chapter Twelve

OEDIPUS: RIDDLE AND DISCOVERY

The story of Oedipus is one of the most familiar and also intriguing of the ancient myths. It was a famous story even as early as Homer's *Odyssey* (11.271–80).[1] Its influence has been monumental, including Sigmund Freud's twentieth-century description of the Oedipus complex. The story of Oedipus reveals fundamental questions about human free will and its relationship to fate and divine will. Oedipus' mysterious fate affects not only himself but also his city of Thebes and his own children, as you will read in the next chapter. The reading here primarily follows the Sophoclean version of the story which has been the most influential.

SOURCES

Homer, *Odyssey* 11.271–80 • Sophocles, *Oedipus the King, Oedipus at Colonus* • Seneca, *Oedipus*

---

1 Homer provides a brief summary of Oedipus' fate, but names Oedipus' mother Epikaste rather than Jocasta, as she is called in later versions.

Thēbae, -ārum, f. pl. - *Thebes*, Greek city in Boeotia
gravidus, -a, -um - *pregnant*
ōrāculum, -ī, n. - *oracle, prophecy*
nātus est: *was born*
servus, -ī, m. - *slave, servant*
5 tālus, -ī, m. - *ankle*
perforō (1) - *to pierce, perforate*
adligō (1) - *to tie, bind*
Cithaerōn, -rōnis, m. - *Mount Cithaeron*, near Thebes
expōnō, -ere, -posuī, -positum - *to expose, abandon*
miserēscō, -ere - *to pity*
Corinthius, -a, -um - *Corinthian, of Corinth*, a Greek city south of Thebes
Meropē, -ēs, f. - *Merope*, wife of Polybus
quibus: dative of possession with a form of *sum, for whom*, translate *who had*
līberī, -ōrum, m. pl. - *children*
orīgō, -ginis, f. - *origin, birth*
occultō (1) - *to hide, keep concealed*
Oedipus, ī, m. - *Oedipus*; in Greek his name means "swollen-foot."
nōminō (1) - *to name*

10 turgidus, -a, -um - *swollen*
Corinthī: locative case (see Wheelock, Ch. 37), *in Corinth*
adolēscō, -ere, -lēvī - *to become mature, grow up*
iuvenis, -is, m. - *a young man, youth*
aliquis, aliquid (pronoun) - *someone, something*
ēbrius, -a, -um - *drunk*
nothus, -ī, m. - *bastard, illegitimate*
falsē: (adv.) - *falsely*
vexō (1) - *to distress, bother, trouble*
iter, itineris, n. - *journey*
15 Delphicus, -a, -um - *Delphic*, of Delphi, the site of Apollo's oracle
Pythia, -ae, f. - *Pythia*, the priestess, seer of Apollo at Delphi
rogātiō, -tiōnis, f. - *question*
nūbō, -ere, nūpsī, nūptum (+ dat.) - *to marry*
victus: *conquered, overcome*
Corinthum: with cities the preposition *ad* may be omitted
redīre: present active infinitive, *to return*
statuō, -ere, -uī, -ūtum - *to decide*
fātum, -ī, n. - *fate*
temptō (1) - *to try, attempt*

Grammar and Comprehension Questions

1) What governs the infinitive *exponēre*?
2) Why is Oedipus saved from death by exposure?
3) To whom does *sibi* refer?
4) How do Polybus and Merope get Oedipus? Why do they adopt him?
5) What case is *Oedipō*? What is its function?
6) What case is *iter*?
7) What tense is *interficiēs*?
8) *What case is timōre?* Why?

Laius erat rēx, Iocasta rēgīna Thēbārum. Diū nūllī puerī eīs erant.
Dēnique Iocasta erat gravida, sed horrendum ōrāculum datum est:
"Fīlius patrem interficiet." Laius igitur fīlium suum timēbat.
Postquam puer nātus est, rēx servum iūssit prīmum tālōs īnfantis
perforāre et adligāre, tum īnfantem in monte Cithaerōne **expōnere**. 5
Servus autem eum miserēscēbat et Corinthiō servō dedit, quī tum
īnfantem Corinthiō rēgī, Polybō, dedit. Polybus et rēgīna Meropē,
quibus nūllī līberī erant, eum fīlium **sibi** adoptāvērunt, sed vēram
orīginem īnfantis occultābant. Īnfantem Oedipum nōmināvērunt,
quod tālī erant turgidī. 10
 Corinthī Oedipus adolēvit. **Oedipō** nunc iuvenī aliquis ēbrius
dīxit: "Tū es nothus." Oedipus īrātus ad parentēs cucurrit et rogāvit:
"Estisne vōs parentēs meī?" Rēx rēgīnaque falsē respondērunt:
"Parentēs sumus." Tamen ille rūmor Oedipum vexābat; **iter** igitur
ad Delphicum ōrāculum fēcit. Pȳthia autem ad rogātiōnem dē vērīs 15
parentibus nōn respondit, sed horrendum ōrāculum dedit: "Patrem
tuum **interficiēs** et mātrī nūbēs." Oedipus **timōre** victus Corinthum
numquam redīre statuit. Sīc fātum vītāre temptābat.

Discussion Questions

1) Consider the exposure of Oedipus on Mt. Cithaeron. What would our society call this?
2) Examine the geographic relationship of Thebes, Corinth, and Delphi on a map. What approximate shape do they make? Where is Mt. Cithaeron?
3) Why do you think Polybus and Merope lied to Oedipus about his birth?
4) The Pythia pronounces Oedipus' fate. Does it make any sense for him to attempt to avoid it?

Delphī, -ōrum, m. pl. - *Delphi*
intereā (adv.) - *meanwhile*
Delphōs: with cities the preposition *ad* may be omitted

20 **quōmodo** (adv.) - *how, in what way*
Sphinx, -ingis, f. - *Sphinx*, a monstrous half-woman, half-bird
Sphingī: dative of separation with *līberāre*.
posset: imperfect tense, subjunctive mood in indirect question construction (see Wheelock, Ch. 30), *he could*
obsideō, -ēre, -sēdī, -sessum - *to besiege, blockade*
conveniō, -īre, -vēnī, -ventum - *to come together, meet*
accēdō, -ere, -cessī, -cessum - *to come near, approach*
currus, -ūs, m. - *chariot*

cēdō, -ere, cessī, cessum - *to yield, withdraw, go*
recūsō (1) - *to refuse*
virga, -ae, f. - *staff, rod*
feriō, -īre, -īvī, -itum - *to strike*
25 **posteā** (adv.) - *afterwards*
etiamnum or **etiamnunc** (adv.) - *still, even now*
excēdō, -ere, -cēdī, -cessum - *to go out, leave, depart*
aenigma, -matis, n. - *riddle, mystery, enigma*
explicō (1) - *to unfold, explain, solve*
māne (adv.) - *in the morning*
pēs, pedis, m. - *foot*
merīdiē (adv.) - *at noon*
vesper, -peris, m. - *evening*
dēvorō (1) - *to swallow down, devour*
30 **grātus, -a, -um** - *grateful*
nōndum (adv.) - *not yet*

Grammar and Comprehension Questions

1) To whom does *eius* refer?
2) What case and function is *eōs*?
3) What person, number, tense, and voice is *victus est*? Give the principal parts of the verb.
4) What tense is *investīgāverant*?
5) Why didn't the Theban citizens investigate Laius' death?

Oedipus Delphōs relīquit et Thēbās ambulābat. Intereā Laius iter
Delphōs faciēbat, quod cupiēbat discere quōmodo Thēbās Sphingī   20
līberāre posset. Nam Sphinx urbem obsidēbat. Ubi trēs viae
conveniunt Oedipus Laium accessit. Laius in currū cēdere viam
Oedipō recūsāvit atque eum virgā ferīvit. Oedipus īrātus rēgem
servōsque **eius** oppugnāvit et interfēcit.

Posteā Oedipus Thēbās accessit quās Sphinx etiamnunc obsidēbat.   25
Nēmō poterat urbem intrāre aut excēdere nisi prīmum aenigma
Sphingis explicāvit: "Quid ambulat māne quattuor pedibus, merīdiē
duōbus, vespere tribus?" **Eōs** quī aenigma nōn explicāvērunt Sphinx
dēvorāvit. Sed Oedipus dē aenigmate putābat. Postrēmō "homō"
respondit. Sīc Sphinx **victus est**. Cīvēs grātī gaudēbant. Nōn sōlum   30
igitur Oedipum rēgem fēcērunt sed etiam Iocastam uxōrem eī
dedērunt. (Cīvēs homicīdium Laiī nōndum **investīgāverant**, quod
Sphinx eōs prohibuerat.)

Discussion Questions

1) Investigate the Pythia and the oracle at Delphi. How did the oracle work? How widely was it believed?
2) Did Oedipus have any justification in attacking and killing Laius?
3) When Oedipus answered the Sphinx' riddle, what happened to the Sphinx? Explore the different mythological variations of the story.

Oedipus solves the riddle of the Sphinx

multōs annōs: accusative of duration of time, *for many years*
35 pestis, -is, f. - *plague, pestilence, disease*
perdō, -ere, -didī, -ditum - *to destroy*
Creōn, -ontis, m. - *Creon*
nūntiō (1) - *to announce, report*
reperiō, -īre, -pperī, -pertum - *to find, discover, learn*
homicīda, -ae, m. - *murderer*
voveō, -ēre, vōvī, vōtum - *to vow, promise*

exsecrātiō, -tiōnis, f. - *curse*
iūrō (1) - *to swear*
quisquis, quisquid - *whoever, whatever*
40 prīdem (adv.) - *long ago*
accidō, -ere, -cidī - *to happen, occur*
Tīresiās, -ae, m. - *Tiresias, the blind Theban prophet*
dēnūntiō (1) - *to threaten*

Grammar and Comprehension Questions

1) What case is *Iocastā?* In what construction?
2) How long do you think Oedipus ruled Thebes before the truth was revealed?
3) What is the hidden family relationship between Oedipus and Creon?
4) What verb form is *reperī?*
5) What irony do you see in Tiresias' prediction for Oedipus?

Tiresias

Oedipus multōs annōs Thēbās bene rēgēbat. Cum
Iocastā duōs fīliōs et duās fīliās generāvit. Dēnique pestis urbem 35
perdēbat. Iterum cīvēs ab Oedipō auxilium petēbant. Oedipus
Creontem, frātrem uxōris, ad ōrāculum mīsit. Creōn tum ōrāculum
nūntiāvit: "**Reperī** homicīdam Laiī." Oedipus homicīdam reperīre
vōvit atque exsecrātiōnem in eum iūrāvit. "Quisquis Laium necāvit,
necesse est hunc in exsilium discēdere et miseram vītam agere." 40
Quoniam iam prīdem homicīdium acciderat, difficile erat homicīdam
invenīre. Oedipus igitur vātem Tīresiam vocāvit, sed prīmō vātēs
dīcere recūsābat. Īrātus rēx vātem dēnūntiāvit. Tīresiās tum īrātus
vēra prōnūntiāvit: "Tū es homicīda quem reperīre temptās. Mox
caecus in oculīs eris ut nunc in mente." Oedipus vātī nōn crēdidit 45
et ipse homicīdium investīgāre coepit.

Discussion Question

1) Why do you think that Tiresias at first refused to speak when summoned by Oedipus?

nūntius, -iī, m. - *messenger*
nūntiō (1) - *to announce, report*
simul (adv.) - *at the same time*

50

accipiō, -ere, -cēpi, -ceptum - *to take, receive, accept*
ōrō (1) - *to beg, beseech*
nē (conj. used with imperative) - *don't*
silēns, -lentis - *silent*

55 perstō (1) - *to persist*
timidē (adv.) - *fearfully*
concēdō, -ere, -cessī, -cessum - *to grant, admit*

miserrimus, -a, -um - *most wretched, most miserable*
ruō, -ere, ruī - *to rush*
quamquam (conj.) - *although*
sērō (adv.) - *too late, late*

60 suspendō, -ere, -pendī, -pēnsum - *to hang, hang up, suspend*
fibula, -ae, f. - *brooch, a metal fastener with a long, sharp point*
vestis, -is, f. - *clothing*
pellō, -ere, pepulī, pulsum - *to strike, push, drive*
efficiō, -ere, -fēcī, -fectum - *to bring about, accomplish*
mendīcus, -ī, m. - *beggar*

Grammar and Comprehension Questions

1) Why did Oedipus feel mixed emotions at the messenger's words?
2) Why did Jocasta enter the house in silence?
3) What tense, person, number, and voice is *vocātus est*?
4) What did Oedipus want to do when he rushed into the house to find Jocasta?
5) To whom does *eius* refer?

Intereā Corinthius nuntius Thēbās advēnit et Oedipō nūntiāvit: "Rēx Polybus mortuus est. Thēbānus populus tē rēgem fēcit." Oedipus mortem Polybī lūgēbat, sed simul gaudēbat quod patrem nōn necāverat. Nūntius autem respondit: "Polybus nōn erat pater tuus. Ē meīs manibus tē īnfantem accēpit." Oedipus rogāvit: "Sed quis est pater mihi? Ā quō mē accēpistī?" Nūntius respondit: "Ā Thēbānō servō." Iam Iocasta Oedipum ōrāvit: "Nē patrem cognōscere pete." Tum silēns rēgīna domum intrāvit. Oedipus autem orīginem petere perstābat. Ille senex, Thēbānus servus, **vocātus est**. Dēnique servus timidē concessit: "Ego tē īnfantem ē manibus Iocastae Laiīque accēpī." Īdem servus etiam homicīdium Laiī vīderat et Oedipum esse homicīdam dēclārāvit. Oedipus, iam miserrimus, in domum ruit. Quamquam rēx Iocastam necāre cupiēbat, eam sērō invēnit. Nam Iocasta sē suspenderat. Oedipus tum fibulās ā vestī **eius** rapuit et hīs ipsīs fibulīs in oculōs suōs pepulit. Sīc Oedipus iam caecus verba Tīresiae effēcit. Nunc etiam propter exsecrātiōnem suam necesse erat Oedipum relinquere Thēbās et mendīcum errāre.

Discussion Questions

1) Does the story of Oedipus' birth and the first prophecy remind you of earlier stories included in this book?
2) How would you characterize Oedipus?
3) Did Oedipus have free will, or was he simply a tool of the gods?
4) How did the process of revelation occur? How many coincidences were involved? Why do you think there were so many?

Cultural Influences

The story of Oedipus has inspired countless works of art, dance, literature, and music. For accounts of literary influence see *Oedipus, Myth and Drama*, ed. Kallich, MacLeish, and Schoenbohm (New York: Odyssey Press, 1968) and Lowell Edmunds, *Oedipus: The Ancient Legend and its Later Analogues* (Baltimore: Johns Hopkins, 1985). A very brief and selective sample of the innumerable works based upon the Oedipus myth follows below:

Art: paintings "Oedipus and the Sphinx" by J. D. Ingres (1808), Gustave Moreau (1864), and Pablo Picasso (1972); Max Ernst, surrealistic painting "Oedipus Rex" (1922).

Dance: ballet by Lully (1664), modern dance *Night Journey* by Martha Graham (1947).

Literature: tragedies by Corneille (1659), Voltaire (1718), Jean Cocteau, *La machine infernale* (1934), Ted Hughes (1968). In 1820 Shelley wrote *Oedipus Tyrannus: or, Swellfoot the Tyrant*, a burlesque satirizing King George IV. Oedipus is even featured in the mystery novel, *The Cat Who Robbed a Bank* by Lilian Jackson Braun (1999).

Music: Incidental music by Purcell (1692), operas by Leoncavallo (1919), Enescu (1921–31), and Orff (1959). Stravinsky's opera-oratorio *Oedipus Rex* (1927) used lyrics by Jean Cocteau which were then translated into Latin.

Oedipus Blinded

© 2006 Christopher J. White

Chapter Thirteen

Oedipus' Further Destiny:
Seven Against Thebes, Antigone

The discovery of Oedipus' true identity and deeds greatly affected both his family and his city. As Oedipus went into exile, a victim of his own curse, his sons Eteocles and Polynices initially shared the rule of Thebes between them; each ruled for one year while the other left the city. Soon, however, there was dissent between the brothers that had tremendous and tragic consequences. This passage describes both the death of Oedipus and the fate of his children.

Sources

Aeschylus, *Seven Against Thebes* • Euripides, *The Suppliants, The Phoeniciean Women* • Sophocles, *Oedipus at Colonus, Antigone* • Seneca, *The Phoenician Maidens*

mendīcus, -ī, m. - *beggar*
multōs annōs: accusative of duration of time (see Wheelock, Ch. 37), *for many years*
fidēlis, -e - *faithful, loyal*
Colōnēus, -a, -um - *of Colonus,* a village near Athens, birthplace of Sophocles
lūcus, -ī, m. - *sacred grove*
Furia, -ae, f. - *Fury,* goddess who takes vengeance, an Avenger; there are usually many.
cognōscō, -ere, -nōvī, -nitum - *to recognize, know*
ōrāculum, -ī, n. - *oracle, prophecy*
meminī, meminisse (defective verb, only in perfect) - *to remember*
Pythia, -ae, f. - *Pythia,* the priestess, seer of Apollo at Delphi

5

praedīcō, -ere, -dīxī, -dictum - *to foretell, prophesy*
placidus, -a, -um - *calm, tranquil, peaceful*
beneficium, -iī, n. - *kindness, favor, benefit*
expellō, -ere, -pulī, -pulsum - *to drive out, expel, banish*
hīc (adv.) - *here*
tandem (adv.) - *at last, finally*
permittō, -ere, -mīsī, -missum (+ dat.) - *to permit, allow*
scelerātus, -a, -um - *wicked, accursed*

10

noceō, -ēre, nocuī, nocitum (+ dat.) - *to do harm to, harm, injure*
ignārus, -a, -um - *not knowing, ignorant*

Grammar and Comprehension Questions

1) In English, what is a mendicant?
2) What is the antecedent of *quō*?
3) What does Oedipus realize when he learns he has come to Colonus?
4) What tense is *accēperint*?
5) How do the citizens react when they learn Oedipus' identity?
6) What case is *scelerāte*?

Oedipus, caecus **mendīcus**, per Graeciam multōs annōs errābat.
Fidēlis fīlia, Antigona, eum dūcēbat. Dēnique ad Colōnēum lūcum
Furiārum advēnērunt. Statim Oedipus locum cognōvit. Nam
ultimum ōrāculum dē sē meminit, in **quō** Pythia mortem Oedipī
praedīxerat: "Post multōs annōs inter Furiās placidum locum veniēs.   5
Ibi beneficia eīs quī tē **accēperint** praebēbis, mala eīs quī te
expulserint." Itaque Oedipus gaudēbat, quod hīc tandem fīnem
labōrum exspectābat. Colōneī cīvēs autem senem timēbant et eī
manēre nōn permittēbant. "Tū, **scelerāte**, discēde; nam scelera
tua nōbīs nocēbunt." At Oedipus dīxit: "Mitte nūntium ad rēgem   10
Thēseum. Rēx mihi manēre permittet, nam Athēnīs magna beneficia
dabō." Oedipus etiam dēclārāvit: "Ignārus scelera commīsī; itaque
innocēns mala tolerō."

Discussion Questions

1) What do you think life would have been like for Antigone as she accompanied Oedipus in exile?
2) How can Oedipus, as a polluted man, offer benefits to anyone?
3) What do you think of the concept that one person's crimes or moral flaws can affect a whole community?
4) Oedipus claims to be innocent of his crimes, since he committed them unknowingly. Do you agree with him?

Ismēnē, -ēs, f. - *Ismene, younger daughter of Oedipus*
15 **maior, maius** - *older*
Eteoclēs, -is, m. - *Eteocles, elder son of Oedipus*
Polynīcēs, -is, m. - *Polynices, younger son of Oedipus*
postulō (1) - *to demand*
exercitus, -ūs, m. - *army*
Argīvus, -a, -um - *Argive, of Argos, an area of Greece in the northern Peloponnesus*
socer, -erī, m. - *father-in-law*
auxilium, -iī, n. - *aid, help*
20
exsecror (1) (deponent verb; see Wheelock, Ch. 34) - *I curse*
maestus, -a, -um - *sad, mournful, grief-stricken*
tonitrus, -ūs, m. - *thunder*
agnōscō, -ere, -nōvī, -nitum - *to recognize*
25 **penitus** (adv.) - *deeply, far within*
subitō (adv.) - *suddenly*
dolor, -lōris, m. - *grief, sorrow*
mīrus, -a, -um - *wonderful, surprising, extraordinary*

modus, -ī, m. - *manner, way*
dux, ducis, m. - *leader, commander, general*
mīles, mīlitis, m. - *soldier*
exsecrātiō, -tiōnis, f. - *curse*
efficiō, -ere, -fēcī, -fectum - *to bring about, accomplish*
30 **proelium, -iī, n.** - *battle*
dēsistō, -ere, dēstitī (+ abl.) - *to leave off, cease*
Creōn, -ontis, m. - *Creon, king of Thebes*
honestus, -a, -um - *noble, honorable*
sepultūra, -ae, f. - *burial*
prōditor, -tōris, m. - *betrayer, traitor*
quisquis, quidquid (indefinite pronoun) - *whoever, whatever*
damnō (1) (+ abl. of penalty) - *to condemn to*
iūssum, -ī, n. - *order, command*
35
Thēbīs: locative case (see Wheelock, Ch. 37), *at/in Thebes*
Haemon, -onis, m. - *Haemon*
spōnsa, -ae, f. - *fiancée*
pāreō, -ēre, -uī (+ dat.) - *to obey*

Grammar and Comprehension Questions

1) What tense, person, and number is *expulistī*?
2) What case is *mīlitēs* and what is its function?
3) Why was Polynices invading Thebes?
4) Why did Oedipus curse his own sons?
5) What case is *Eteoclī* and what is its function?
6) How does Oedipus' death compare to the end of most human lives? What was unusual about Oedipus' death?

Oedipus' Further Destiny

Intereā, Ismēnē, minor fīlia Oedipī, advēnit et gravem rēm
nūntiāvit. Eteoclēs, maior fīlius Oedipī, frātrem Polynīcem expulerat. 15
Īrātus Polynīcēs rēgnum sibi postulābat atque exercitum contrā
Thēbās ēdūcēbat. Adrastus, Argīvus rēx et socer, cōpiās Polynīcī
parābat. Iam Polynīcēs ad Oedipum vēnit. Nam ōrāculum audīverat
atque auxilium patris cupiēbat. At Oedipus auxilium eī recūsāvit.
Dīxit: "Tū mē, patrem tuum, caecum miserumque ex urbe **expulistī**. 20
Nunc mendīcus errō. Nunc et tē fratremque tuum exsecror: frater
fratrem in bellō interficiet." Polynīcēs iam maestus discēssit.

Iam Thēseus advēnerat et senem accēperat. Statim Oedipus
magnum tonitrum audīvit et signum deī agnōvit. Cum Thēseō in
lūcum penitus recessit. Ibi Oedipus subitō sine dolōre ā vītā discessit. 25
Thēseus sōlus mīrum modum mortis vīdit.

Mox Polynīcēs Thēbās oppugnāvit. Septem ducēs **mīlitēs** contrā
septem portās ducēbant. Polynīcēs portam quam Eteoclēs dēfendēbat
oppugnābat. Duo frātrēs exsecrātiōnem patris effēcērunt: frāter
frātrem interfēcit. Tum aliī cīvēs et hostēs proeliō dēstitērunt. Creōn 30
imperium iam habēbat. Omnibus nuntiāvit: "**Eteoclī**, quī prō patriā
mortuus est, honestam sepultūram dabimus, sed Polynīcī, quī
prōditor urbem nostram oppugnāvit, nūllam sepultūram permittam.
Quisquis hoc iūssum negleget, hunc morte damnābō."

Antigona iam Thēbīs vīvēbat atque Haemonī, fīliō Creontis, 35
spōnsa erat. Illa autem iūssō pārēre recūsāvit;

Discussion Questions

1) What do you think of Polynices continuing the attack on Thebes despite the curse of his father? What attitude does this reveal toward his allies?
2) What did the Greeks believe about the importance of burial? What happened to the soul of a person who was unburied?

cōnstāns, -antis - *standing firm, resolute*
humō (1) - *to bury*
40   manipulus, -ī, m. - *handful*
pulvis, -veris, m. - *dust*
spargō, -ere, spārsī, spārsum - *to scatter over, spread, strew*
custōs, -tōdis, m. - *guard*
spārsum: neuter accusative singular, perfect passive participle (see Wheelock, Ch. 23), *strewn, sprinkled*
furō, -ere - *to rage with anger, rave*
45   ferōx, -rōcis - *defiant*
decus, -coris, n. - *honour, esteem, glory*
lēx, lēgis, f. - *law*
50   spēlunca, -ae, f. - *cave, cavern*
inclūdō, -ere, -clūsī, -clūsum - *to shut in, enclose*

lamentātus, -a, -um - *wept over, lamented*
monitiō, -tiōnis, f. - *admonition, warning*
rītus, -ūs, m. - *rite, ceremony*
55   victus, -a, -um - *conquered, overcome*
sērō (adv.) - *too late, late*
suspendō, -ere, -pendī, -pēnsum - *to hang, hang up, suspend*
amplexābātur: third person singular imperfect of deponent verb (see Wheelock, Ch. 34), *was embracing*
Eurydicē, -ēs, f. - *Eurydice*
incūsō (1) - *reproach, blame, censure, accuse*
60   homicīda, -ae, m. - *murderer*
līberī, -ōrum, m. - *(one's) children*
dolor, -ōris, m. - *grief, sorrow*
diūtius (comparative adv.) - *longer*

Grammar and Comprehension Questions

1) What is interesting about the gender of *illum*? To whom does it really refer?
2) What case and function is *mortālia iūssa*?
3) What case and number is *sōlī* and what does it modify?
4) What tense is *suspenderat*?
5) How is Antigone similar in fate to her mother Jocasta?

Ismēnem igitur iuvāre rogāvit. Ismēnē autem respondit: "Nōs fēminae sumus. Quid nōs facere possumus?" Antigona tum īrāta cōnstānsque Polynīcem clam humāvit, nam inter tempestātem tribus manipulīs pulveris corpus spārsit. Mox custōs corpus pulvere spārsum invēnit et rēgī nūntiāvit. Creōn tum furēbat et iterum **illum** quī corpus humāverat morte damnābat. Antigona etiamnunc cōnstāns corpus iterum humāvit. Īdem custōs eam prope corpus invēnit et eam ad Creontem dūxit. "Haec est quae iūssum tuum violāvit." Ferōx Antigona nōn sōlum culpam nōn negāvit sed etiam decus sēnsit. Creontī dīxit: "Dīvīnae lēgēs sunt aeternae et **mortālia iūssa** superant." Creōn autem eam morte damnāvit. Haemon ōrāvit: "Cīvēs puellam clam laudant. Thēbae tibi **sōlī** nōn sunt. Sī spōnsam meam interficiēs, multa mala inveniēs." Sed Creōn obstinātus custōdēs iūssit: "Hanc scelerātam ad spēluncam dūcite et inclūdite." Sīc Antigona ā cīvibus lāmentāta ad mortem ambulāvit. Dēnique Tīresiās advēnit et horrendam monitiōnem nūntiāvit. "Deī sacrificia nostra recūsant, quod tū dīvīnās lēgēs violās. Sī puellam nōn līberābis et Polynīcem plēnīs rītibus humābis, mox tū fīlium tuum āmittēs." Tandem Creōn, terrōre victus, corpus humāvit; posteā Antigonam līberāre temptāvit sed sērō. Nam Antigona sē **suspenderat**. Haemon in spēluncā corpus spōnsae amplexābātur. Īrātus fīlius prīmum patrem gladiō oppugnāre temptāvit, tum sē interfēcit. Miser Creōn duo corpora domum portāvit. Ibi uxor Eurydicē rēgem incūsāvit et eum homicīdam līberōrum vocāvit. Tum Eurydicē sē gladiō interfēcit. Creōn dolōre victus est. Domus Oedipī nōn diūtius erat.

Discussion Questions

1) The name Antigone means "one who struggles against." How does her name reflect her role?
2) Antigone gives her life to bury her brother. Why was proper burial so important to her? Why did she bury the body twice?
3) Examine ancient burial practices. How do they compare to modern ones?

Cultural Influences

See especially George Steiner, *Antigones* (Oxford U. Press, 1984) which discusses the influence of Sophocles' *Antigone* on western literature.

Art: marble statue by William Henry Rinehard "Antigone Pouring a Libation over the Corpse of Her Brother Polyneices" (1867–70); marble sculpture group "Oedipus at Colonus" with Antigone by Jean-Baptiste Hugues (1882–85); sculptures and etchings by Leonard Baskin (1946–71); George de Chirico "Oedipus and Antigone" as mannequin figures in a surrealistic painting (1950–68); "Antigone et Créon," drawing by Jean Cocteau (1923); Mark Rothko painting "Antigone" (1938). "Eteocles and Polyneices" painting by Tiepolo (c. 1725–30); Antonio Canova "Lament for Eteocles and Polyneices," terra-cotta sculpture group (c. 1798–99).

Drama: Jean Cocteau, *Antigone* (1923); Jean Anouilh, *Antigone* (1942); Bertolt Brecht, *Die Antigone des Sophokles* (1948); T. S. Eliot verse drama based on *Oedipus at Colonus* "The Elder Statesman" (1958); *Gospel at Colonus*, gospel-music adaptation of *Oedipus at Colonus* produced by Lee Breuer with the Five Blind Boys of Alabama (1984), available on videotape from PBS; *Antigone*, film produced by George Tsavellas (1961).

Music: Franz Schubert "Antigone and Oedipus," song (1817); Felix Mendelssohn, incidental music to *Antigone* (1841) and *Oedipus at Colonus* (1845); ballet *Antigone* by Mikis Theodorakis (1959). Operas *Antigone* by Scarlatti (1756), Honegger (1900), Saint-Saens (c. 1850), and Orff (1959).

Oedipus led by Antigone

Chapter Fourteen

The Birth of Hercules

Hercules (Heracles in Greek) is the most famous Greek hero. His legend is so extensive that it would require a book in itself. This chapter and the next feature, first, his extraordinary birth and childhood and, second, the twelve labors that have come to characterize him. The hero's name means "glory of Hera," which is odd because, as you will read, it was Hera (Juno in Latin) who was his enemy and forced him to undergo many trials. The goddess was jealous and vengeful because Jupiter had fallen in love with Alcmena, a mortal woman. Almena was the wife of the hero Amphitryon who lived in Thebes but was of Argive royal blood. Hercules was Alcmena's child by Jupiter. In the end Hercules proved his worth and was accepted by the goddess as a demi-god at his death.

The passage below begins when Amphitryon was away at battle while Alcmena at home anxiously awaited his return.

Sources

Homer, *Iliad* 19.96–133 • Hesiod, *Shield of Heracles* 1–59 • Pindar, *Nemean Odes* 1. 41–72 • Theocritus, *Idylls* 24 • Plautus, *Amphitryon* • Ovid, *Metamorphoses* 9.280–323

fidēlis, -e - *faithful, loyal*
Amphitryon, -ōnis, m.
  - *Amphytryon,* king of Thebes
speciēs, -ēī, f. - *appearance, look*
adsūmō, -ere, -sumpsī, -sumptum
  - *to take to oneself, assume*
domus, -ūs, f. - *house, home*
coniūnx, -ugis, m. - *husband*
salūtō (1) - *to welcome, greet*
5 suscēnseō, -ēre, -uī - *to be angry, indignant*
hesternus, -a, -um - *of yesterday*
stupefactus, -a, -um - *stunned, amazed*
quōmodo (adv.) - *how, in what way*
venia -ae, f. - *forgiveness, pardon*
10
inviðeō, -ēre, -vīdī, -vīsum (+ dat.)
  - *to be jealous of, feel ill will toward*
aemula, -ae, f. - *rival (in love)*
Herculēs, -is, m. - *Hercules* (the Greek Heracles)
pariō, -ere, peperī, partum - *to produce, give birth to*

sēmen, -minis, n. - *seed, stock, race*
nāscētur: third person singular future of deponent verb (see Wheelock, Ch. 34), *will be born*
modus, -ī, m. - *manner, way*
15 Sthenelus, ī, m. - *Sthenelus,* king of Mycenae
perfectus, -a, -um - *complete*
Lūcīna, -ae, f. - *Lucina,* goddess of childbirth, equivalent to the Greek Eileithyia
partus, -ūs, m. - *birth, childbirth*
iūssum, -ī, n. - *order, command*
necesse (indeclinable adj.) - *necessary*
necesse est: takes accusative and infinitive, *it is necessary that*
Eurystheus, -ī, m. - *Eurystheus,* son of Sthenelus
dētineō, -ēre, -tinuī, -tentum - *to retard, delay*
20 pertineō, -ēre, -tinuī - *to pertain, apply to*

Grammar and Comprehension Questions

1) What case is *illā nocte?* What is its function?
2) How does Jupiter deceive the faithful Alcmena?
3) What tense and voice is *facta est?*
4) Why is Amphitryon surprised?
5) What case, number, and gender is *eī?* What is its function?
6) To whom does *aemulae* refer?
7) What case is *hōc modō* and what is its function?
8) How does Juno deceive Jupiter?
9) What form is *audī?*

Iuppiter Alcmēnam amābat, sed Alcmēna erat fidēlis uxor
Amphitryōnis. Deus igitur speciem Amphitryōnis adsumpsit et
domum eius intrāvit. Laeta Alcmēna coniugem salūtāvit. **Illā nocte**
Alcmēna ē Iove gravida **facta est**. Mox Amphitryōn ipse etiam
domum advēnit et suscēnsēbat quod uxor sē nōn cito salūtāvit. 5
Alcmēna respondit: "Sed tū hesternā nocte advēnistī. Tum tē salūtāvī."
Amphitryōn, stupefactus et īrātus, rogāvit: "Quōmodo herī advenīre
poteram, quoniam herī magnum bellum gerēbam?" Alcmēna fidem
eī iūrāvit et deinde Amphitryōn veniam uxōrī dedit. Tum Alcmēna ē
Amphitryōne etiam gravida facta est. 10
Iūnō mortālī fēminae, quam Iuppiter amāverat, invidēbat. Dea
fīlium **aemulae** dēlēre cupiēbat. Dum Alcmēna īnfantem Herculem
parere temptat, Iuppiter iūrāvit: "Hodiē puer sēmine meō nāscētur.
Hic omnēs hominēs reget." Iūnō autem Iovem **hōc modō** dēcēpit.
Alia fēmina, uxor Sthenelī, etiam gravida ē Iove erat, sed tempus 15
nōndum perfectum erat. Tamen Iūnō dīxit Lūcīnae, deae partūs:
"Mea iūssa **audī**. Hodiē necesse est uxōrem Sthenelī parere Eurystheum,
sed etiam necesse est Alcmēnam nōn parere Herculem." Lūcīna igitur
labōrem Alcmēnae dētinuit sed partum Eurystheī accelerāvit. Sīc verba
Iovis ad Eurystheum nōn Herculem pertinēbant. 20

Discussion Questions

1) What kind of marital relationship do Jupiter and Juno seem to have?
2) Jupiter as a sky god is also a fertility god. How is this characteristic of Jupiter featured in the story?

geminus, -ī, m. - *twin*
Iphiclēs, -is, m. - *Iphicles*
cūnābula, -ōrum, n. - *cradle*
dormiō, -īre, -īvī, -ītum - *to sleep*
25 excitō (1) - *to rouse, wake*
vāgiō, -īre, -īvī - *to wail, utter cries of distress*
vāgītus, -ūs, m. - *cry of distress, wail, howl*
immō (particle) - *on the contrary, rather*
prehendō, -dere, -dī, -sum - *to take hold of, grasp*

30 cubiculum -ī, n. - *bedroom*
mīrus, -a, -um - *wonderful, surprising, extraordinary*
spectāculum, -ī, n. - *spectacle, sight*
sedeō, -ēre, sēdī, sessum - *to sit*
rīdeō, -ēre, rīsī, rīsum - *to laugh, smile*
vātēs, -is, m. - *prophet, seer*
praenūntiō (1) - *to announce in advance, prophesy*
efficiō, -ere, -fēcī, -fectum - *to bring about, accomplish*

Grammar and Comprehension Questions

1) How long did Alcmena endure labor?
2) What sound effect is created by *vāgīvit*? What is the term for this effect?
3) What in Iphicles' behavior reveals his mortal parentage?
4) What case and function is *serpentēs*?
5) Who is the subject of *vīdit*?

Sed misera Alcmēna septem diēs labōrābat. Deinde octāvō diē geminōs puerōs, Herculem et Iphiclem peperit. Iam Iūnō īnfantem Herculem necāre temptāvit. Duōs ingentēs ācrēsque serpentēs in geminōs mīsit. Īnfantēs in cūnābulīs dormiēbant. Iphiclēs ē somnō sē excitāvit et terrōre **vāgīvit**. Vāgītus frātris Herculem excitāvit. 25
Sed Herculēs nōn timēbat; immō **serpentēs** manibus prehendit et strangulāvit. Intereā Amphitryōn vāgitūs audīvit, gladium prehendit, et in cubiculum cucurrit. Ibi mīrum spectāculum **vīdit**: Herculēs sedēbat et ante sē duōs mortuōs serpentēs tenēbat. Īnfāns etiam rīdēbat et patrī serpentēs praebēbat. Tum Amphitryōn vēritātem 30
intellēxit: Herculēs erat vērus fīlius Iovis. Vātēs Tīresiās quoque praenūntiāvit: "Mox Herculēs magnīs factīs magnam glōriam sibi sed etiam magnum dolōrem efficiet."

Discussion Questions

1) Consider the relationship as indicated in the story between the gods and humans. How would you describe it?
2) What is the character of Juno as revealed in the passage?
3) What does the prophecy of Tiresias imply about the achievement of glory?
4) Consider the figure of Tiresias. How often have you seen him before? How old do you think he is?

Cultural Influences

Art: Filarete, "The Infant Hercules," relief on bronze door of St. Peter's, Rome (1433–45); Joshua Reynolds, "The Infant Hercules (Strangling the Serpents)," painting (1786–88); William Blake, "The Infant Hercules Throttling the Serpents," drawing (c. 1790–93); Horace Greenough, relief depicting infant Hercules on side of chair of "Washington," marble sculpture (1832–41); Paul Manship, "Infant Hercules Fountain," bronze, American Academy, Rome (1914).

Chapter Fifteen

THE LABORS OF HERCULES

The goddess Hera, implacably hostile to Hercules, caused him to murder his own children in a fit of madness. When he realized what he had unwittingly done, Hercules fled to the oracle at Delphi. The oracle told him that he could atone for the murders if he served his cousin Eurystheus, king of Tiryns, for twelve years. During that period Hercules performed twelve labors, in most of which Hercules rid the earth of dangerous animals. The completion of these labors also brought him immortality. In addition to these labors, many more feats throughout the known world were attributed to the hero, since every town wanted to establish some connection with the hero. The account below gives some details about each of the famous twelve labors.

SOURCES

Homer, *Odyssey* 11.601–26 • Hesiod, *Theogony* 327–33 • Sophocles, *Women of Trachis* 1092–1100 • Theocritus, *Idylls* 25, especially 162ff. • Vergil, *Aeneid* 6. 801–03 • Diodorus Siculus, *Biblioteca* (Library) 4.3–26

Herculēs, -is, m. - *Hercules (the Greek Heracles)*
Nemeaeus, -a, -um - *Nemean, of Nemea, a valley in Argolis, in the Greek Peloponnesus*
leō, -ōnis, m. - *lion*
pellis, -is, f. - *hide, skin*
referō, -ferre, -ttulī, -lātum - *to bring back*
saxeus, -a, -um - *rocky*
rīma, -ae, f. - *narrow cleft, crack, fissure*
claudō, -ere, clausī, clausum - *to shut, close*
sagitta, -ae, f. - *arrow*
integer, -gra, -grum - *untouched, whole, unhurt*
5   **aes, aeris, n.** - *bronze*
ferrum, -ī, n. - *iron*
clāva, -ae, f. - *club, knotty staff*
pulsō (1) - *to strike, beat*
attonitus, -a, -um - *stunned*
tergum, -ī, n. - *back*
scandō, -ere, scandī, scānsum - *to climb, mount*
unguis, -is, m. - *nail, claw*
10 **dētrahō, -ere, -traxī, -tractum** - *to take away, remove, skin*
gestō (1) - *to wear*
quandōcumque (adv.) - *whenever, as often as*
Lernaeus, -a, -um - *Lernean, of Lerna, a marsh in Argolis*

hydra, -ae, f. - *hydra, a many-headed water snake*
venēnātus, -a, -um - *poisonous*
serpentem: here, feminine
15
crēscō, -ere, crēvī, crētum - *to come into existence, arise, grow*
Iphiclēs, -is, m. - *Iphicles, half-brother of Hercules*
patruus, -ī, m. - *father's brother, paternal uncle*
quotiēnscumque (adv.) - *however often, whenever*
vulnus, -eris, n. - *wound*
adūrō, -ere, -ūssī, -ūstum - *to set fire to, singe, cauterize*
saxum, -ī, n. - *rock, stone*
tingō, -ere, tinxī, tīnctum - *to wet, moisten*
20
aper, aprī, m. - *wild boar*
Erymanthus, -ī, m. - *Erymanthus, a chain of mountains in Arcadia in Greece*
vīvus, -a, -um - *alive, living*
niveus, -a, -um - *snowy, white*
persecūtus est: deponent verb (see Wheelock, Ch. 34), translate actively, [he] *chased*.

Grammar and Comprehension Questions

1) What case is *Herculī*?
2) What implements did Hercules first use against the lion?
3) Why did Hercules have to kill the Nemean lion by strangulation? Why did he use the lion's claws to skin it?
4) What case is *unguibus* and why?
5) What becomes the symbol of Hercules?
6) What does Hercules do with the blood of the hydra?

The Labors of Hercules

I. Rēx Eurystheus prīmum labōrem **Herculī** dēclārāvit: "Nemeaeum leōnem interfice et pellem ad me refer." Hic leō erat ingēns et in saxeā rīmā vīvēbat. Prīmum Herculēs exitum rīmae clausit. Deinde sagittam in leōnem mīsit, sed leō integer remanēbat! Nam neque aes neque ferrum illam pellem penetrāre poterat. Herculēs igitur caput leōnis ingentī clāvā pulsāvit. Breviter leō attonitus erat. Statim Herculēs tergum leōnis scandit et duābus manibus leōnem strangulāvit. Herculēs mortuum leōnem ad Eurystheum portāvit, quī territus fūgit. Tum Herculēs pellem **unguibus** leōnis ipsīus dētraxit. Nam unguēs poterant pellem penetrāre. Posteā Herculēs pellem semper gestābat, quod pellis eum dēfendēbat. Quandōcumque pictūram Herculis vidēs, clāvam et pellem leōnis etiam vidēs.

II. Secundus labor erat interficere Lernaeam hydram, venēnātam serpentem, quae plūrima capita habēbat quōrum ūnum caput erat immortāle. Ubi Herculēs ūnum caput amputāvit, ibi duo capita statim crescēbant. Tum Iolāus, fīlius Iphiclis, patruum adiuvābat. Quotiēnscumque Herculēs caput amputāvit, Iolāus vulnus adūssit. Dēnique Herculēs immortāle caput amputāvit et sub magnō saxō posuit. Tum sagittās in sanguine hydrae tinxit; itaque sagittae venēnātae factae sunt.

III. Tum Eurystheus iūssit Herculem: "Ingentem aprum in Erymanthō monte cape et eum vīvum ad me redūc." Herculēs aprum in niveum agrum persecūtus est.

Discussion Questions

1) We no longer believe in mythological hydras. What is a hydra today and where would you find one?
2) What is a boar? What is so dangerous about it? Examine the role of boars in mythology. For instance, read the story of Meleager and the boar.

altus, -a, -um - *high, deep*
nix, nivis, f. - *snow*
rēte, -is, n. - *net*

25

cerva, -ae, f. - *hind, female deer*
Ceryneus, -a, -um - *Cerynean, of Cerynea, related to Mount Lyceus in Arcadia*
necesse est: takes acccusative and infinitive **tē capere.**
sacer, -cra, -crum (+ dat.) - *sacred (to)*
aereus, -a, -um - *of bronze*
pēs, pedis, m. - *foot*
cervae: dative of possession, *the deer had...*
noceō, -ēre, -uī, -itum (+ dat.) - *to do harm to, harm, injure*
poscō, -ere, poposcī - *to demand, require*
stringō, -ere, strinxī, strictum - *to graze, injure*

30

prōmittō, -ere, -mīsī, -missum - *to promise*
perficiō, -ere, -fēcī, -fectum - *to complete, accomplish*
ignōscō, -ere, -nōvī, -nōtum (+ dat.) - *to forgive, pardon*
quīntus, -a, -um - *fifth*

avis, -is, f. - *bird*
Symphālius, -a, -um - *Stymphalian, of a lake in Arcadia*
lacus, -ūs, m. - *lake*
edō, edere, ēdī, ēsum - *to eat*

35

penna, -ae, f. - *feather*
fremitus, -ūs, m. - *roaring, noise*
crepitāculum, -ī, n. - *rattle*
ēvolō (1) - *to fly out, forth*
percutiō, -ere, -cussī, -cussum - *to strike through*
Augēās, -ae, m. - *Augeas, king of Elis in Greece*
stabulum, -ī, n. - *stable*
equus, -ī, m. - *horse*
pūrgō (1) - *to clean, wash*

40

dēflectō, -ere, -flexī, -flexum - *to turn aside, divert*
sextus, -a, -um - *sixth*
īnstituō, -ere, -stituī, -stitūtum - *to establish, set up, institute*
extrā (adv.) - *outside*

45

taurus, -ī, m. - *bull*
Diomēdēs, -is, m. - *Diomedes, king of Thrace*

50

soleō, -ēre, solitus sum - *to be accustomed to*

Grammar and Comprehension Questions

1) How did Hercules tire the boar?
2) What tense, person, and number is *nocēbō*?
3) What tense, person, and number is *perfēcerō*?
4) What is the antecedent of *quibus*?
5) What form is *purgāta erant*?
6) Why did Eurystheus send Hercules outside Greece beginning with the sixth labor?
7) What is the antecedent of *quī*? Hint: look at the following verb.

The Labors of Hercules — 115

Mox aper altā nive fatīgātus est. Herculēs igitur eum rētī capere
poterat. Sīc erat tertius labor. 25

IV. Deinde Eurystheus iūssit: "Cervam Ceryneam necesse est tē
capere." Cerva erat celeris et sacra Diānae; etiam aerea cornua et
aereī pedēs erant cervae. Herculēs cōgitābat: "Sī cervae **nocēbō**,
dea poenam ā mē poscet." Tamen Herculēs cervam sagittā strinxit
et in tergō suō portābat. Statim īrāta Diāna poenam poposcit, sed 30
Herculēs Eurystheum culpābat. Herculēs autem prōmīsit: "Cervam
līberābō, sī labōrem **perfēcerō**." Diāna igitur eī ignōvit.

V. Nunc Eurystheus quīntum labōrem iūssit—interficere avēs quae
silvās prope Stymphālium lacum vexābant. Avēs hominēs edēbant;
pennās autem ut sagittās iacere poterant. Herculēs magnum fremitum 35
crepitāculō fēcit et avēs terruit, quae tum ēvolāvērunt. Tum Herculēs
eās sagittīs percussit et sīc interfēcit.

VI. Rēx Augēās vasta stabula habēbat in **quibus** multī equī vīvēbant.
Haec stabula numquam **pūrgāta erant**. Itaque Eurystheus Herculem
iūssit stabula pūrgāre. Labor vīsus est īnfīnītus. Sed Herculēs duo 40
flūmina dēflexit, quae tum per stabula fluēbant. Postquam hunc sextum
labōrem perfēcit, Herculēs Olympiōs lūdōs in honōrem Iovis īnstituit.

VII. Nunc Eurystheus hērōem extrā Graeciam mīsit, quod omnia
mōnstra in Graeciā iam interfecta erant. Eurystheus Herculem
trāns mare in Crētam mīsit. "Magnum taurum Crētae cape" 45
Eurystheus iūssit. In Crētā Herculēs taurum superāvit et in tergō
eius trāns mare ad Graeciam portātus est. Postquam Herculēs
taurum Eurystheō dēmōnstrāvit, eum līberāvit.

VIII. Deinde Eurystheus Herculem iūssit equōs rēgis Diomēdis
capere, **quī** in Thrāciā habitābant et hūmānōs edere solēbant. 50

custōs, -tōdis, m. - *guard*
agō, -ere, ēgī, actum - *to drive, lead*
persecūtus est: perfect tense, deponent verb (see Wheelock, Ch. 34), *pursued, chased*
vorō (1) - *to swallow, devour*
diūtius (adv.) - *longer*
ferus, -a, -um - *wild, uncivilized, fierce*
55 **ulterius** (adv.) - *further*
zōna, -ae, f. - *belt,* traditionally known as a girdle; broad band worn around the waist
Amāzonius, -a, -um - *of the Amazons,* warrior women of the east

dōnō: dative after *dēderat, for a gift, as a gift*
hospes, -pitis, m. - *guest*
inveniō, -īre, -vēnī, -ventum - *to intervene, interfere*
60 **longē** (adv.) - *far*
occidēns, -ntis - *western*
bōs, bovis, m. - *bull, ox, cow;* plural, *cattle*
Gēryōn, -yonis, m. - *Geryon,* a monstrous king in Spain
pōculum, -ī, n. - *drinking-vessel, cup, bowl*

Grammar and Comprehension Question

1) What case is *bellum?* What is its function?

Amazon warrior

Herculēs custōdēs equōrum superāvit et equōs ad mare ēgit.
Diomēdēs eum persecūtus est; sed Herculēs rēgem interfēcit, quī
tum ab equīs suīs vorātus est. Posteā equī nōn diūtius erant ferī.
Itaque Herculēs equōs ad Eurystheum sine perīculō dūxit.

IX. Deinde Eurystheus Herculem ulterius, ad Asiam, mīsit. Fīlia 55
Eurystheī zōnam Amāzoniae rēgīnae, Hippolytae, cupiēbat. Mars,
pater Hippolytae, zōnam dōnō dēderat. Prīmō rēgīna Herculem
hospitem accipiēbat et zōnam prōmīsit, sed Iūnō intervēnit et **bellum**
incēpit. Hippolyta interfecta est, cuius zōnam Herculēs tum cēpit.

X. Nunc Eurystheus Herculem longē ad occidentem īnsulam mīsit. 60
Herculem iūssit bovēs Gēryonis rapere, cui tria corpora erant.
Canis eius autem duo capita habēbat. Apollō hērōem iuvāvit, nam
eī aureum pōculum dedit, in quō Herculēs ad īnsulam nāvigāvit.

Hercules and the Hydra

65 impōnō, -ere, -posuī, -positum - *to place in*

ōra, -ae, f. - *edge, border*

mālum, -ī, n. - *apple*

Hesperidēs, -um, f. pl. - *the Hesperides,* women who lived in the farthest western land. (Hesperus means "west" in Greek.)

hortus, -ī, m. - *garden*

custōdiō, -īre, -īvī, -ītum - *to guard*

nuptiālis, -e, *of a wedding, marriage*

70

patefaciō, -ere, -fēcī, -factum - *to disclose, reveal*

Atlās, -lantis, m. - *Atlas,* a Titan

orbis, -is, m. - *circle*

orbis terrārum: *the world, earth*

sustineō, -ēre, -uī, -tentum - *to hold up, sustain*

libenter (adv.) - *gladly*

consentiō, -īre, -sēnsī, -sēnsum - *to agree, assent*

75 dēiciō, -ere, -iēcī, -iectum - *to put down*

tandem (adv.) - *at last, finally*

pondus, -deris, n. - *weight, burden*

paulum (adv.) - *a little*

parumper (adv.) - *for a short while, a moment*

80 rīdeō, -ēre, rīsī, rīsum - *to laugh, smile*

ōstium -iī, n. - *door, entrance*

īnferī, -ōrum, m. pl. - *those below, the dead, the underworld*

85 Plūtō, -ōnis, m. - *Pluto,* ruler of the underworld

arma, -ōrum, n. - *arms, weapons*

pithus, -ī, m. - *pithos,* a large storage jar big enough for an adult to hide in

saliō, -īre, saluī - *to leap, jump*

hūc (adv.) - *here, to here*

posthāc (adv.) - *after this*

90 servitūs, -tūtis, f. - *servitude, slavery*

Grammar and Comprehension Questions

1) What gender, number, and case is *quae*? What is its antecedent?
2) How did Hercules trick Atlas?
3) What form is *iuvātus* and what does it modify?
4) How did Eurystheus react when he saw Cerberus?

Hercules, Athena, and Cerberus

Ibi Herculēs Gēryonem canemque interfēcit; tum bovēs in pōculum
imposuit et ad Eurystheum revēnit.

XI. Mox Eurystheus herōem ad occidentem ōram terrae iterum mīsit.
Iūssit: "Aurea māla Hesperidum ad mē portā." In hortō ingēns serpēns
centum capitibus custōdiēbat haec māla, **quae** Gāia Iūnōnī nuptiālī
dōnō dederat. Prīmō Herculēs locum hortī invenīre nōn poterat.
Herculēs locum hōc modō invēnit: vīcit deum maris, Nēreum, quī
sē in plurimās fōrmās mūtāre poterat. Victus Nēreus locum patefēcit.
Prope hortum Herculēs Tītānum Atlantem invēnit, quī orbem
terrārum sustinēbat. Herculēs Atlantī dīxit: "Sī māla mihi capiēs,
orbem terrārum tibi sustinēbō." Atlās libenter cōnsēnsit et mox māla
rettulit. Sed Atlās orbem terrārum iterum sustinēre recūsābat.
Herculēs itaque discēdere nōn poterat, nam orbem terrārum dēicere
nōn audēbat. Tandem Herculēs Atlantem hōc modō dēcēpit: "Pondus
orbis umerōs meōs paulum dolet. Sī orbem terrārum parumper
recipiēs, tum pondus ferre parābō." Atlās māla dēposuit et orbem
terrārum iterum recēpit. Sed Herculēs rīsit et cum mālis fūgit.

XII. Dēnique ultimum labōrem Eurystheus iūssit. Quod omnēs
labōrēs in terrā perfectī erant, Eurystheus Herculem ad Tartarum
mīsit. "Cerberum ad mē redūc." Cerberus erat canis tribus capitibus
quī ōstium īnferōrum custōdiēbat. Herculēs ā Mercuriō Minervāque
iuvātus in Tartarum dēscendit. Ibi Plūtōnem ōrābat. Plūtō respondit:
"Permittō tibi canem redūcere, sī eum sine armīs capere potes."
Manibus sōlīs canem Herculēs superāvit et ad Eurystheum redūxit.
Ingēns canis Eurystheum terruit, quī in magnum pithum statim
saluit. Tum Eurystheus hērōī clāmāvit: "Numquam hūc posthāc vēnī."
Sīc servitūs Herculis perfectus est. Hērōs canem ad Plūtōnem redūxit.
Post mortem suam Herculēs deus factus est.

Discussion Questions

1) What similarities do many of the labors share? What is the effect of the successful completion of the labors for others besides Hercules?
2) Hercules is often considered to have more brawn than brains. Do his labors require any intelligence or merely strength?
3) What is the derivation of the word "atlas"?
4) Use an atlas to trace the travels of Hercules during his labors.
5) Research the Olympian games. What was the traditional date of their founding?
6) The passage above contains a number of mythological names which provide the basis for English words. How many English words can you find that derive directly from these? (Hint: there are at least five.)
7) The Stoic philosophy greatly admired Hercules. What about his behavior provides a positive example?
8) The derivation of the word Stoicism is interesting. You can find it in the dictionary. How do you explain it?

Cultural Influences

Hercules' labors have probably inspired more interpretations in art, literature, and music than any other ancient myth. The works included below are only a very small selection.

Art: There are many ceiling frescoes and groups of illustrations of the labors. See Filarete, relief of Hercules and the Nemean lion on the bronze doors of St. Peter's, Rome (1433–35); Antonio del Pallaiuolo, bronze statuette "Hercules" (1478–80); Raphael, engraving *Heracles strangling the Nemean Lion* (1520); several paintings by Rubens (c. 1615); Lucas Cranach "The Labors of Hercules" painting cycle (after 1537); Michelangelo, drawings of *Three Labors of Hercules* (c. 1530); Paolo Veronese represents Hercules as strength in "Allegory of Wisdom and Strength," painting (c. 1570); Giambologna "Hercules with a Club," bronze statuette (c. 1580); Peter Paul Rubens, "Head of Hercules," painting (c. 1611); Sebastiano Ricci frescoes depicting the labors (1706–7); John Singer Sargeant, *Hercules and the Hydra*, mural (1921–25); Eugene Delacroix, "Hercules resting from his Labors," painting (1858); Giorgio de Chirico painting *Hercules* (1953).

Literature: Hercules' labors retold in "The Monk's Tale" in Chaucer's *Canterbury Tales* (c. 1388); Shakespeare, Hercules in the Pageant of Nine Worthies in *Love's Labor's Lost* (1594–95); Marianne Moore, "The Labors of Hercules" poem (1935); Archibald MacLeish, "Herakles" verse drama (1967).

Music: many operas including by Ariosti (1703), Vivaldi (1723), and even a musical comedy by Richard Rodgers *By Jupiter!* (1942); composition for piano by Louis Moreau Gottschalk (1869).

Hercules Strangles the Nemean Lion

Chapter Sixteen

Jason's Quest for the Golden Fleece

The fame of Jason, the hero from Thessaly in northern Greece, has continued undiminished into the twenty-first century. Indeed his name is often still given to children. Like Hercules and Theseus, Jason's myth includes many exploits. This selection will feature the expedition of his Argonauts, which took place in the generation before the Trojan War. Many heroes with special powers, such as Orpheus, accompanied Jason.

Jason's father Aeson had been King of Iolchus but had been deposed by his younger half-brother Pelias. Thus Jason grew up secretly in exile. Pelias had been warned by a prophecy that a stranger wearing only one sandal would harm him. When Jason became an adult, he travelled to Iolchus to claim the throne from Pelias. On his journey he came to a raging river, beside which an old woman stood. Although others had refused to help her, Jason carried her across, but in the process he lost one sandal. The old woman was in fact the goddess Juno (Hera) in disguise. Juno thus became Jason's protector.

When Jason arrived in Iolchus he was unrecognized. His uncle Pelias, however, noted his missing sandal and remembered the prophecy. Jason then revealed his identity and demanded that Pelias surrender power to him. Pelias, eager to get rid of Jason, answered that he would surrender the throne, provided that Jason brought him the golden fleece. The fleece came from a ram, sent by the gods, which had rescued Pelias' cousins Phrixus and Helle by flying them to safety from Iolchus and the murderous plots of their step-mother. The ram landed in far-off Colchis on the remotest stretch of the Black Sea. Phrixus then hung the fleece in a shrine. Since no ship had ever sailed as far as Colchis, Pelias assumed that Jason would be killed in the attempt. Jason, undaunted, and with Minerva's help, built the first sea-going ship and assembled a crew of heroes who, after many adventures, finally arrived in Colchis. This episode begins when Jason asks King Aeetes of Colchis to give him the fleece, which he claims is rightly the property of his family. The language of the passage is based primarily on Ovid, particularly from *Heroides* 12.

Sources

Hesiod, *Theogony* 992–1002 • Pindar, *Pythian Ode* 4 • Euripides, *Medea* • Apollonius of Rhodes, *Argonautica*, especially Book 3 • Theocritus, *Idyll* 22.45–136 • Diodorus Siculus, *Universal History* 4. 40.1–5 • Ovid, *Heroides* 6, 12; *Metamorphoses* 7.1–400

Aeētēs, -is, m. - *Aeetes*, king of Colchis
peregrīnus, -a, -um - *foreign, alien;* here used as a substantive, *foreigners*
Iāsōn, -sonis, m. - *Jason*
Argonautae, -ārum, m. pl. - *Argonauts,* heroes who sailed on the Argo with Jason
Colchis, -chidis, f. - *Colchis,* city on the eastern coast of the Black Sea
vellus, -eris, n. - *fleece, sheepskin*
5 pretium, -iī, n. - *price, value*
magnī pretiī: genitive of valuation, *of great value, worth*
exportō (1) - *to carry out, take away*
facilē (adv.) - *easily*
perficiō, -ere, -fēcī, -fectum - *to complete, accomplish*
explicō (1) - *to explain*
dūrus, -a, -um - *hard, harsh, rough, hardy*
collum, -ī, n. - *neck*

ferus, -a, -um - *wild, uncivilized, fierce*
premō, -ere, pressī, pressum - *to press, press hard*
insolītus, -a, -um - *unfamiliar, unaccustomed, strange*
vōmer, -meris, m. - *ploughshare,* thus *plough, yoke*
insolītō vōmere: ablative, *at the unfamiliar plough, yoke*
aereus, -a, -um - *made of bronze*
nāris, -is, f. - *nostril*
10 adflātus, -ūs, m. - *breathing, breath*
dēns, dentis, m. - *tooth*
lātus, -a, -um - *broad, wide*
sēmen, -minis, n. - *seed*
armātus, -a, -um - *armed, furnished with weapons*
mīles, mīlitis, m. - *soldier*
persuādēbat: takes the dative
nē (conj.) - with imperative, *don't*

Grammar and Comprehension Questions

1) What attitude does Aeetes have towards foreigners? What is the term for this?
2) What claim does Jason think he has to the golden fleece?
3) What is the case and function of *labōrēs*?
4) What tense, person, number, and voice is *factae sunt*? With what does *factae* agree?
5) How do you translate *ut* in this clause? What kind of literary device is this?
6) What form is *temptā*?

Aeētēs, fīlius Sōlis, erat saevus rēx quī peregrīnōs praesertim ōdit.
Postquam Iāsōn et Argonautae Colchidem advēnērunt, Iāsōn ad
Aeētem statim vēnit et rogāvit: "Aureum vellus mihi dā, quod est
gentī meae." Sed Aeētēs vellus dare recūsāvit, quod erat magnī
pretiī. Rēx igitur sīc respondit: "Tibi vellus exportāre permittam, 5
sī **labōrēs**, quōs ego facile perficere possum, perficere poteris."
Tum labōrēs explicāvit. "Prīmum necesse est dūra colla ferōrum
taurōrum premere insolītō vōmere. Nam taurī sunt Martis, quōrum
terribilis spīritus est ignis. Pedēs sunt aereī. Etiam aereae nārēs
adflātibus suīs nigrae **factae sunt**. Deinde tē iubeō dentēs serpentis 10
per latōs agrōs spargere. Mox dentēs, **ut** sēmina, generābunt armātōs
mīlitēs, quī tē interficere temptābunt. Necesse est tē omnēs mīlitēs
interficere." Sīc Aeētēs dīxerat et omnēs Argonautae territī Iāsonī
persuādēbat: "Nē labōrēs **temptā**, nam nūllō modō hōs perficere poteris.

Discussion Questions

1) Why could Aeetes handle fire-breathing bulls without being burnt?
2) Why does Jason believe he is entitled to get the golden fleece?
3) What is unusual about the crop that Jason must sow? (You may want to compare this myth with the foundation myth of Thebes. There Cadmus sowed the teeth of the same dragon or serpent.)

15 **rēgnum, -ī, n.** - *kingdom*
Iolchus, -ī, f. - *Iolchus, seaport city in Thessaly in northern Greece*
recipiō, -ere, -cēpī, -ceptum - *to gain possession of, get back*
perniciōsus, -a, -um - *deadly, destructive*
auxilium, -iī, n. - *aid, help*
Mēdēa, -ae, f. - *Medea, her name means "clever, cunning."*
sacerdōs, -dōtis, f. - *priestess*
Hecatē, -ēs, f. - *Hecate, an earth goddess associated with black magic; often identified with Diana*
20 **iūssū:** *by order of*
Cupīdō, -inis, m. - *Cupid, the son of Venus; the love god*
trānsfīgō, -ere, -fīxī, -fīxum - *to pierce through*
somnium, -iī, n. - *dream*
nēquīquam (adv.) - *in vain, uselessly*
fidēlitās, -tātis, f. - *fidelity, loyalty, faithfulness*
ergā (prep. + acc.) - *towards, for*
distrahō, -ere, -traxī, -tractum - *to pull apart, tear*

āit - *he/she says*
25 **certē** (adv.) - *certainly*
tantus, -a, -um - *so large, so great*
modo (adv.) - *just, only, merely*
30 **celeriter** (adv.) - *swiftly, quickly*
timidē (adv.) - *timidly, fearfully, shyly*
patefaciō, -ere, -fēcī, -factum - *to make open, disclose, reveal*
libenter (adv.) - *with pleasure, gladly*
praetereā (adv.) - *moreover, in addition*
grātus, -a, -um - *grateful, thankful, appreciative*
nūbere: *takes the dative*
occultus, -a, -um - *hidden, secret, occult*
lūna, -ae, f. - *moon*
dētrahō, -ere, -traxī, -tractum - *to draw down, pull down*
tollō, -ere, sustulī, sublātum - *to raise, lift up*
cōgō, -ere, coēgī, coāctum - *to compel*
retrō (adv.) - *backwsards*
medicāmentum, -ī, n. - *drug*

Grammar and Comprehension Questions

1) What case is *sagittā* and what is its function?
2) What is the antecedent of *quibus*?
3) How does Medea initially react to her unexpected love for Jason?
4) What tense, person, and number is *dederō*?
5) Where do Medea and Jason secretly meet?
6) Why is Medea able to help Jason with magic?
7) What case and number is *medicāmenta*? What is its grammatical function?

Fortis Iāsōn respondit: "Sine vellere rēgnum Iolchī recipere nōn 15
poterō. Quamquam labōrēs videntur perniciōsī, tamen necesse est
mē eōs temptāre."
Auxilium autem mox aderat. Mēdēa, fīlia rēgis et sacerdōs
Hecatēs, vīdit Iāsonem et statim saevō amōre vincēbātur. Nam
deae Iūnō Venusque Iāsonem iuvāre cupiēbant. Iūssū deārum 20
igitur Cupīdō Mēdēam **sagittā** amōris trānsfīxit. Tum Mēdēa malīs
somniīs vexābātur in **quibus** Iāsōn labōrēs nēquīquam temptābat.
Mēdēa inter amōrem et fidēlitātem ergā patrem distrahēbātur.
Dēnique Mēdēa amōrem vincere nōn poterat et sibi āit: "Nēquīquam,
Mēdēa, repugnās. Certē hoc est quod amor vocātur. Nam cūr iūssa 25
patris nimium dūra mihi videntur? Cūr est tantus timor hospitis
quem modo vīdī? Nisi auxilium eī **dederō**, taurī et mīlitēs eum
interficient." Itaque Mēdēa nūntium ad Iāsonem clam mīsit: "Venī
ad templum Hecatēs. Auxilium tibi dabō." Iāsōn ad templum
celeriter vēnit. Mēdēa amōrem timidē patefēcit et auxilium praebuit. 30
Iāsōn libenter auxilium accēpit; praetereā grātus bellae puellae
nūbere prōmīsit. Sacerdōs Mēdēa multās occultās artēs cognōvit:
lūnam dē caelō dētrahere, mortuōs ē Tartarīs tollere, cōgere flumina
retrō fluēre. Itaque Mēdēa nova **medicāmenta** Iāsonī parāvit.
Sacerdōs docuit: "Haec medicāmenta corpus tuum ab ignī dēfendent 35
et magnam vim per ūnum diem praebēbunt." Mēdēa etiam Iāsonem
sōlum vincere omnēs mīlitēs docuit.

Discussion Questions

1) Why does Jason persist in what seems an impossible and fatal challenge?
2) Why do the goddesses choose Medea, a young girl, to help Jason?
3) What does Jason promise Medea in return for her help?
4) What are some of Medea's special skills?

clipeus, -ī, m. - *shield*
linō, -ere, lēvī, litum - *to smear, coat*
potestās, -tātis, f. - *power, ability*

40

dux, ducis, m. - *leader, commander, general*
ecce (interjection) - *behold! look!*
aeripēs, -pedis - *bronze-footed*
herba, -ae, f. - *grass, plants*
tactus, -a, -um - *touched*
ardeō, -ēre, arsī - *to catch fire, burn*
findō, -ere, fīdī, fissum - *to cleave, split apart*

45

medius, -a, -um - *middle; the middle of*
poscō, -ere, poposcī - *to ask for, demand;* takes double accusative of person and thing

50

nemus, -moris, n. - *grove, wood*
dormiō, -īre, -īvī, -ītum - *to sleep*
sopiō, -īre, -īvī, -ītum - *to overcome with sleep, put to sleep*
rāmus, ī, m. - *branch* (of a tree)
ūnā (adv.) - *together*

55

prōdō, -ere, -didī, -ditum - *to betray*

Grammar and Comprehension Questions

1) What happens when the bulls breathe on the grass?
2) What case and construction is *ā Iāsone*?
3) What does Jason throw into the midst of the soldiers?
4) What case is *vellus* and what is its function?
5) Who actually overcame the serpent?
6) What is the subject of *dedērunt*?

Nunc diēs labōrum aderat. Iāsōn tōtum corpus et clipeum medicāmentīs lēvit. Statim magnam vim potestātemque sentiēbat. Ad agrum vēnit, ubi multī spectātōrēs eum exspectābant. 40 Argonautae prō duce suō praesertim timēbant. Rēx ipse ingentēs taurōs ēmīsit. Ecce aeripedēs taurī ē nāribus ignem exhālant. Herbae ignī tāctae ardent. Sed Iāsōn salvus stat. Taurōs iungit et terram vōmere findit. Tum agrum dentibus serpentis ut sēminibus implet. Mox dentēs ā **Iāsone** iactī sē in armātōs mīlitēs mūtant. 45 Statim mīlitēs Iāsonem oppugnant. At Iāsōn ā Mēdēā monitus magnum saxum in mediōs mīlitēs iacit. Mīlitēs nunc inter sē pugnant, et citō omnēs mortuī sunt. Sīc Iāsōn labōrēs perfēcit. Itaque Aeētem **vellus** poposcit. Aeētēs autem etiamnunc recūsābat.

Iterum Mēdēa Iāsonem iuvāre statuit. Nocte Iāsōn Mēdēaque 50 ad occultum nemus advēnērunt, in quō vellus magnō serpente servābātur. Quamquam serpēns numquam ante dormīverat, tamen Mēdēa mōnstrum medicāmentīs sopīvit. Deinde Iāsōn vellus dē rāmō rapuit. Iāsōn Mēdēaque ad nāvem ūnā cucurrērunt. Argonautae Iāsonem vellusque vīdērunt et gaudēbant. Citō vēla ventīs **dedērunt** 55 et Colchidem relīquērunt. Cum eīs Mēdēa, quae patrem patriamque prō Iāsone prōdiderat, nāvigābat.

Discussion Questions

1) How does Jason succeed in single-handedly defeating an entire army?
2) How does Jason capture the golden fleece?
3) In helping Jason Medea betrays her father. What other mythological character acts similarly?

Cultural Influences

Art: Filarete, "Jason" and "Jason and the Argonauts" reliefs on bronze door, St. Peter's, Rome (1433–35); paintings by Utili, "The Meeting of Jason and Medea" (1486–87); Ercole da Ferrara, "Jason Kills the Dragon before Medea" (1496); Joseph Turner "Jason" as he confronts the dragon (1802); Gustave Moreau "Jason," taking the fleece with Medea (1865); Maxfield Parrish "Quest of the Golden Fleece" (1908); Giorgio de Chirico, "The Departure of the Argonauts" (1909, 1922); Max Ernst, "The Argonauts," abstract painting (1933).

Film: *Jason and the Argonauts* (1963), dir. Don Chaffey; NBC TV–movie by the same name, dir. Nick Willing (2000).

Literature: Lope de Vega, *El Vellocino de Oro*, drama (1622); Pierre Corneille, *La conquete de la Toison d'Or*, tragedy (1660); Richard Glover, *Jason*, tragedy (1785); Andrew Lang, "The Story of the Golden Fleece," children's story (1903); Robert Graves, *Hercules, My Shipmate* (first published as *The Golden Fleece)*, novel (1944).

Music: several operas and cantatas beginning with Cavalli's 1648 opera, *Il Giasone*.

Jason and Medea

Chapter Seventeen

MEDEA'S VENGEANCE

This chapter continues the complicated story of Jason and Medea. King Aeetes realized that Jason would not have been able to accomplish the feats and steal the golden fleece without Medea's help. Recognizing Medea's betrayal, he pursued the Argonauts to reclaim both the fleece and his daughter. There are various versions of the pursuit. In Apollonius of Rhodes, Medea's younger brother Apsyrtus led the pursuit. Jason sent him a message saying that he would return Medea if Apsyrtus met him in private. When Apsyrtus arrived, Jason then killed him. Centuries later Cicero and Ovid report that Medea had taken Apsyrtus with her (a strange choice for a woman desperately in love). To escape from her pursuing father, Medea killed Apsyrtus and chopped his body into pieces, which she threw upon the waves. Aeetes, horrified, stopped to pick up the pieces of his son. The delay allowed Medea and Jason to escape. Whichever version one believes, Medea felt responsible for the death of her brother and the betrayal of her father (see Euripides' *Medea* 166–67).

After eluding their pursuers, Jason and Medea returned to Greece by a circuitous route, during which they were married by Circe, a goddess-witch who was Aeetes' sister. When they arrived in Iolchus, King Pelias was still unwilling to relinquish power to Jason or his father. Once again Medea tried to help Jason. With her magical powers she rejuvenated Jason's father, Aeson. She further demonstrated her skill to the daughters of Pelias by turning an old ram into a young lamb. The daughters of Pelias naively asked Medea to help rejuvenate their father as well. The daughters cut up their father, but Medea gave no restorative potions and so the king was dead. Medea's plan, however, backfired. Horrified by her actions, the citizens of Iolchus exiled Jason and Medea. Eventually the couple came to Corinth, where King Creon allowed them to stay. When the action begins, Medea has borne Jason two children and the family has been welcomed and accepted by the neighbors. Jason, however, has new plans. This chapter is based primarily on Euripides' *Medea*.

SOURCES

In addition to the sources cited in the previous chapter, see Seneca's tragedy, *Medea*. The Latin vocabulary in this chapter is based upon Ovid's *Heroides* 12 and *Metamorphoses* 7.

Iāsōn, -ōnis, m. - *Jason*
Corinthus, -ī, f. - *Corinth,* a city in Greece
Corinthī: locative case (see Wheelock, Ch. 37), *in Corinth*
parum (adv.) - *too little*
peregrīnus, -ī, m. - *foreigner*
potestās, -tātis, f. - *power, influence*
status, -ūs, m. - *rank, standing, prestige*
coniūnx, -ugis, f. - *partner in marriage,* here *wife*
5 Creōn, -ontis, m. - *Creon,* king of Corinth (not the Creon of Thebes featured in the Oedipus legend)
marītus, -ī, m. - *husband*
celeriter (adv.) - *swiftly, quickly*
10 prōditiō, -tiōnis, f. - *betrayal*
maestus, -a, -um - *sad, mournful, grief-stricken*
cibus, -ī, m. - *food*

Corinthius, -a, -um - *of Corinth, Corinthian*
adlevō (1) - *to comfort, console*
ōrō (1) - *to beg, beseech*
deōs mortem ōrābat: a double accusative of the gods invoked and the thing prayed for
dēserō, -ere, -uī, -itum - *to abandon, desert*
prōdō, -ere, -didī, -ditum - *to betray, forsake*
15 omnia: nominative neuter plural, *everything,* to be taken with *marītus ... sōlus*
nihil: adverbial, *not at all*
amārus, -a, -um - *bitter*
vigilō (1) - *to be awake*
tener, -era, -erum - *tender, delicate, soft*
absum, -esse, -fuī, -futūrus - *to be absent, away from*

Grammar and Comprehension Questions

1) What case is *Mēdēae* and what is its function?
2) How did Medea learn of Jason's new plans?
3) How did Medea behave when she first learned of Jason's desertion?
4) What tense and voice is *prōditae sunt*? With what does *prōditae* agree?
5) What tense is *faciam*?
6) Why is *ego* included when the personal ending of the verb indicates the subject?

Nunc Iāsōn Mēdēaque Corinthī habitābant. Iāsōn autem parum
contentus erat, quod ut peregrīnus nūllam potestātem, nūllum
statum tenēbat. Etiam Mēdēa, coniūnx eius, erat barbara; itaque
fīliī eōrum cīvēs esse nōn poterant. Iāsōn autem pulcher erat et
nōbilis. Creōn, rēx Corinthī, marītum fīliae suae petēbat. Dēnique   5
Creōn Iāsonem fīliae suae nūbere rogāvit. Quamquam coniūnx
fīliique Iāsonī iam erant, Iāsōn celeriter hoc mātrimōnium accēpit.
Mēdēae nihil dīxit.
   Sed nūntius ad Mēdēam vēnit et dē novō mātrimōniō nuntiāvit.
Prīmum Mēdēa hanc prōditiōnem crēdere nōn poterat. Sed tum   10
maesta miseraque dēspērābat; cibum aquamque etiam recūsābat.
Fīliōs suōs vidēre nōn cupiēbat. Amīcae, fēminae Corinthiae, eam
adlevāre temptābant, sed Mēdēa deōs mortem ōrābat. Sibi Mēdēa
dīcēbat: "Dēseror. Patria domusque ā mē **prōditae sunt**—nēquīquam!
Marītus, quī sōlus mihi omnia erat, mē relīquit prōdiditque.   15
Serpentēs taurōsque vincere potuī, sed ūnum virum tenēre nōn
potuī. Nihil artēs meae iuvāre possunt. Diēs mihi nōn grātus est;
per amārās noctēs vigilō et tener somnus ā miserō pectore abest.
Quid **faciam**? Quae spēs est? Virum, quem **ego** servāvī, alia
fēmina mox tenēbit."   20

Discussion Questions

1) What bothered Jason about his situation in Corinth?
2) Why could Jason's children not become Corinthian citizens?

maga, -ae, f. - *sorceress, witch*

noceō, -ēre, -uī, -itum (+ dat.) - *to do harm to, harm, injure*

25 quō (adv.) - *to where?/ whither?*

quōmodo (adv.) - *how, in what way*

cūrō (1) - *to care for*

vertō, -ere, vertī, versum - *to turn, change*

concēdō, -ere, -cessī, -cessum - *to grant, allow*

fortasse (adv.) - *perhaps*

30 iniūria, -ae, f. - *injury, wrong*

mīrē (adv.) - *strangely*

vindicō (1) (with *in* + accusative) - *to take vengeance against, to punish*

35

nupta, -ae, f. - *bride*

dīxissem: pluperfect tense, subjunctive mood (see Wheelock, Ch. 30) in a past contrary-to-fact condition (see Wheelock, Ch. 33): *if I had spoken.*

invidia, -ae, f. - *jealousy, envy*

prūdentia, -ae, f. - *wisdom, discretion, prudence, good sense*

vīcisset: pluperfect tense, subjunctive mood of *vincō*, concluding the condition: *would have conquered.*

castīgō (1) - *to berate, castigate*

40 sīcine (interrogative adv.) - *in this way?* (with indignant force)

prōditor, -tōris, m. - *betrayer, traitor*

Symplēgādēs, -um, f. pl. - *Symplegades*, two enormous rocks at the entrance to the Black Sea which crushed ships which attempted to pass through. Only divine intervention prevented the Argo from being crushed.

ēlīdō, -ere, ēlīsī, ēlīsum - *to crush*

tālis, -e - *such*

possēmus: imperfect tense, subjunctive mood (see Wheelock, Ch. 29) in a present contrary-to-fact condition (see Wheelock, Ch. 33): *we would not be able.*

fraus, -dis, f. - *deceit, treachery*

crēdulitās, -tātis, f. - *credulity, gullibility*

Grammar and Comprehension Questions

1) Do you recognize the enclitic ending of *Mēdēaene?* What is its meaning?
2) What does Creon fear Medea might do?
3) To whom is Medea speaking in the quote that follows *sē rogāvit?*
4) What does Jason offer Medea? What are her feelings about his offer?
5) What does Medea claim she did for Jason?
6) What case is *quibus* and what is its function?
7) What case and time construction is the phrase *ūnō diē?*
8) What is the antecedent of *quam?*
9) What tense is *dēfendent?*

Rēx Creōn Mēdēam timēbat, quod cognōvit eam esse potentem magam. Rēx cōgitābat: "**Mēdēane** fīliae meae nocēbit?" Creōn igitur ad Mēdēam vēnit et dēcrēvit: "Necesse est tē fīliōsque tuōs ē rēgnō meō statim discēdere. Nam īram tuam timeō." Nunc iterum Mēdēa dolōre victa est. **Sē rogāvit**: "Quō fugiam? Quae terra mē accipiet? Quōmodo puerōs meōs cūrābō?" Tum ad Creōntem vertit et ōrāvit: "Ūnum diem mihi concēde. Prō mē nōn labōrō sed prō fīliīs, **quibus** domum invenīre temptābō." Creōn respondit: "Saevus nōn sum. Quamquam fortasse errō, tamen hunc diem dabō. Nam **ūnō diē** nūllam iniūriam perficere poteris. Sī autem crās tē in hōc rēgnō vidēbō, mīlitēs meī tē interficient." 25

30

Postquam Creōn discessit, Mēdēa mīrē gaudēbat. Nam nunc in rēgem, fīliam, et Iāsonem vindicāre dēcrēvit.

Mox Iāsōn intrāvit. Pecūniam Mēdēae fīliīsque praebuit, **quam** īrāta Mēdēa recūsāvit. Iāsōn sē excūsābat: "Hoc novum mātrimōnium tibi fīliīsque nostrīs fēcī. Nova nupta enim puerōs generābit, quī tum frātrēs suōs **dēfendent**. Sī autem hoc cōnsilium tibi dīxissem, invidia prūdentiam tuam vīcisset. Nam tū saepe es īrāta." Tum īrāta Mēdēa Iāsonem castīgābat: "Quis tē servāvit? Ego, ut omnēs Graecī sciunt. Sīcine prō vītā tuā grātiam agis? Prōditor! Ubi nunc deī sunt, per quōs iūrāvistī? Crēdisne hōs deōs nōn iam esse? Symplēgādēs nāvem ēlīsisse debuērunt; nam nunc tālēs poenās dare nōn possēmus, tū poenās fraudis, ego crēdulitātis. Discēde!" 35

40

Discussion Questions

1) Why does Creon exile Medea?
2) What are Medea's options as an exile? What would her life be like? Could she support her children?
3) What fatal mistake does Creon make?
4) What flaw does Medea find in Jason's justification for his behavior? What do you think of his explanation? What do you think a Greek audience felt?

perfugium, -iī, n. - *refuge*

līberī, -ōrum, m. pl. - *(one's) children*

Delphicus, -a, -um - *of Delphi, a Greek city famous for the oracle of Apollo*

aenigma, -matis, n. - *enigma, riddle*

explicō (1) - *to explain, solve*

paenitēre: *to be regretful, to regret*

simulō (1) - *to pretend, feign*

ignōscō, -ere, -nōvī, -nōtum (+ dat.) - *to forgive*

cōnsentiō, -īre, -sēnsī, -sēnsum - *to agree*

sapienter (adv.) - *wisely*

stola, -ae, f. - *robe*

diadēma, -matis, n. - *ornamental headband, crown*

placeō, -ēre, -uī, -itum (+ dat.) - *to please*

Grammar and Comprehension Questions

1) What tense is *rogāverat*?
2) Why did Aegeus consult the Delphic oracle?
3) What case and function are *haec dōna*?

Medea contemplates the murder of her children

Dum Mēdēa perfugium invenīre temptābat, amīcus Aegēus, rēx
Athēnārum, advēnit. Nam cōnsilium doctae Mēdēae petēbat. 45
Nūllī līberī erant Aegēō. Itaque Delphicum ōrāculum **rogāverat**:
"Quōmodo līberōs prōdūcere poterō?" Ōrāculum responderat,
sed respōnsum erat aenigma. Mēdēa aenigma explicāvit; grātus
Aegēus eī perfugium praebuit.
 Iam Mēdēa novum et terribile cōnsilium poenae parābat. 50
Iāsonem vocāvit et paenitēre simulābat. "Tum īra mē vīcit. Dēbēs
mihi ignōscere, quod sōlum fēmina sum. Nunc cōnsentiō: tū
sapienter haec cōgitābās. Ego in exsilium discēdam. Sed prō fīliīs
meīs labōrō. Itaque **haec dōna** novae nuptae accipe. Ecce hanc
bellam stolam et diadēma. Sī haec dōna eī placēbunt, fortasse fīliī 55
nostrī in hōc rēgnō manēre poterint. Nam nupta tua rēgī persuadēbit."
Iāsōn cōnsēnsit.

Discussion Question

1) How and why does Aegeus' visit cause Medea to change her plan of vengeance?

ācer, ācris, ācre - here, *bitter, terrible* 70
venēnum, -ī, n. - *poison*
tingō, -ere, tinxī, tinctum - *to wet, imbue*
60 rēgia, -ae, f. - *palace*
invidus, -a, um - *hostile*
āvertō, -ere, -vertī, -versum - *to turn away, avert*
sūmō, -ere, sūmpsī, sūmptum - *to take, take up* 75
speculum, -ī, n. - *mirror*
identidem (adv.) - *again and again, repeatedly*
titubō (1) - *to stagger*
vestis, -is, f. - *clothing*
frustrā (adv.) - *in vain, uselessly*
adhaereō, -ēre, -haesī, -haesum (+ dat.) - *to adhere to, stick to*
ardeō, -ēre, arsī - *to burn, blaze*
65 viscera, -um, n. pl. - *internal organs, inner parts*
īnscius, -a, um (+ gen.) - *ignorant, unknowing*

maximē (adv.) - *especially, most greatly*
pūniō, -īre, -īvī, -ītum - *to punish*
laedō, -ere, laesī, laesum - *to injure, harm, hurt*
aspiciō, -ere, -spexī, -spectum - *to look at, behold*
renūntiō (1) - *to renounce, call off*
num (interrogative adv.) - introduces questions which expect the answer "no"
rīdeō, -ēre, rīsī, rīsum - *to laugh, laugh at*
hōc ūnō diē: ablative of time within which, *for* . . .
dēdiscō, -ere, -dicī - *to forget, put out of one's mind*
magnopere (adv.) - *greatly, exceedingly*
odium, -iī, n. - *hatred*

Grammar and Comprehension Questions

1) Does the princess welcome Medea's children?
2) What are the principal parts of the verb *cecidit*?
3) What case and function is *clāmōrēs*?
4) Why does Medea groan at the news of her children's reprieve from exile?
5) Why is *vīcērunt* plural?

Medea's Vengeance

Tum Mēdēa duōs fīliōs vocāvit et bella dōna in manūs puerōrum posuit. Sed prīmum dōna ācrī venēnō tinxerat.

Mox puerī ad rēgiam vēnērunt. Invida fīlia rēgis oculōs ā 60
puerīs āvertit; at dōna eī placēbant. Statim nupta stolam diadēmaque sūmpsit et sē in speculō identidem spectābat. Subitō autem puella titubāvit et clāmāvit et vestem removēre temptābat—frustrā, nam stola diadēmaque corporī adhaerēbant. Nunc dōna flammīs ardent quae viscera puellae dēvorant. Dēnique fīlia venēnō victa est et ad 65
terram **cecidit**. Sed pater, īnscius malī, **clāmōrēs** fīliae audīvit et ad eam cucurrit. Fīliam tollere temptābat, sed mox pater ipse eōdem venēnō captus est.

Intereā nūntius ad Mēdēam vēnit: "Puerī tuī sunt salvī: rēx eōs hīc manēre permittet." Tum Mēdēa gemuit, quod nunc ultimam 70
partem poenae perficere necesse erat. Nam Mēdēa fīliōs suōs interficere statuerat, quod sīc maximē Iāsonem pūnīre et laedere poterat. Sed tum Mēdēa oculōs et ōra puerōrum aspexit et cōnsilia renuntiāvit. "Fīliōs meōs laedere nōn possum. Etiam sī Iāsonem laedam, ego ipsa semper puerōs dolēbō. Nunc amor īram vincit." 75
Sed tum Mēdēa dē hostibus cōgitābat: "Num permittam hostibus meīs rīdēre mē? Nōn. Necesse est hōc ūnō diē mē dēdiscere cārōs fīliōs meōs. Posteā eōs semper dolēre poterō." Sīc, quamquam māter fīliōs magnopere amābat, tamen odium Iāsonis et cupiditās poenae amōrem **vīcērunt**. Duōs fīliōs gladiō interfēcit. 80

Discussion Questions
1) How can the children handle the poisoned gifts and remain unharmed?
2) Examine the character of the step-mother in Greek mythology. For instance, see Ino.

domum: as with the names of cities the preposition *ad* may be omitted
recipiō, -ere, -cēpī, -ceptum - *to take back, regain*
sērō (adv.) - *too late, late*
potius (adv.) - *rather*
tundō, -ere, tutudī, tūnsum - *to strike with repeated blows, beat*
īnsum, -esse, -fuī, -futūrus - *to be inside, within*
immō (particle) - indicates strong contrast, *no indeed, rather*
tectum, -ī, n. - *roof*
currus, -ūs, m. - *chariot*

85 **dracō, -ōnis, m.** - *snake, large serpent*
tractātus, -a, -um - *drawn, pulled*
adstō, -stāre, -stitī - *to stand by*
plōrō (1) - *to weep aloud, wail, lament*
humō (1) - *to bury*
sit: present tense, subjunctive mood in indirect question (see Wheelock, Ch. 30), translate *is*
rēiciō, -ere, -iēcī, -iectum - *to reject*
90 **gignō, -ere, genuī, genitum** - *to bear, produce*
ēvolō (1) - *to fly away, off*

Grammar and Comprehension Questions

1) Why did Jason rush back to his house?
2) What case is *domūs*?
3) Where did Jason find Medea?
4) What person, number, and tense is *effēcistī*?
5) What gender and number is *quae*? What is its antecedent?
6) Who will bury the children?

Mox Iāsōn mala facta Mēdēae cognōvit et domum cucurrit. Poenās ā Mēdēā petēbat et fīliōs recipere cupiēbat - sed sērō. Potius novum malum invēnit. Iāsōn portās **domūs** tutudit, sed Mēdēa nōn inerat. Immō in tectō stābat et corpora fīliōrum tenēbat. Currus sōlis dracōnibus tractātus adstābat. Iāsōn corpora vīdit et plōrāvit: 85
"Quid scelus **effēcistī**, ō mala fēmina? Omnēs deī tē ōdērunt **quae** haec scelera facis. Dā mihi corpora cārōrum fīliōrum meōrum quōs dolēbō et humābō." Mēdēa respondit: "Dēī cognōvērunt quem culpāre necesse sit. Nunc eōs amās quōs tum rēiciēbās. Discēde! Novam nuptam humā! Meōs fīliōs ego humābō, ego quae eōs genuī 90 amōque." Tum in currū ēvolāvit. Miser Iāsōn relictus est.

Discussion Questions

1) Euripides does not give the princess a name, although in other accounts she is called Glauke or Creusa. Why do you think Euripides leaves her nameless? How is she characterized?
2) Why did Medea decide to kill her children?
3) In other versions it is the Corinthian citizens who killed the children to take vengeance against Medea. Why do you think Euripides makes Medea kill them?
4) How does Medea escape from Corinth? Why do the gods let Medea go unpunished for the multiple murders?
5) What is a *deus ex māchinā*? Does Medea fulfill this role?

Cultural Influences

Art: Peter Paul Rubens, "The Flight of Medea," drawing (1640); Rembrandt "Medea," etching (1648); Jean-Francois de Troy, studies for tapestry series on the myths of Medea and Jason (1742–46); French School, Gobelins tapestries including "Creusa Consumed by the Fire of the Fatal Dress Presented by Medea" (1789); Joseph Turner, "Vision of Medea," painting (1828); Eugene Delacroix, "Medea about to Kill Her Children," painting (1838); Frederick Sandys, "Medea" (mixing poison), painting (1868); Auguste Rodin, "Medea" (holding child), sculpture (1865–70); Paul Cézanne, "Medea," watercolor after Delacroix (1880–85); series of sculptures, drawings, and paintings by Leonard Baskin (1976–82).

Film: Pier Paolo Pasolini, *Medea* (1968) with Maria Callas; Jules Dassin, *A Dream of Passion* (1978) with Ellen Burstyn and Melina Mercouri; authentic production with masks of Euripides' play in ancient Greek with English subtitles by The New York Greek Drama Company (1986).

Literature: Geoffrey Chaucer, "The Legend of Hypsipyle and Medea," part of *The Legende of Goode Women* (1385–86); tragedies *Médée* by Pierre Corneille (1634–35) and Jean Anouilh (1946).

Music: many ballets, cantatas, and operas, especially Luigi Cherubini, *Médée*, opera (1797) and Darius Milhaud (1938); Samuel Barber, *Cave of the Heart*, orchestral suite to accompany the ballet of same title by Martha Graham (1946–47).

Medea's Vengeance

Medea Kills Her Children

Chapter Eighteen

Leda and the Swan: The Birth of Helen, Clytaemnestra and the Dioscuri

The Romans thought their chief god, Jupiter, was equivalent to the Greek Zeus. There were, however, significant differences between the two. Greek mythology gave greater emphasis to Zeus' role as a fertility god and thus depicted his many liaisons with women, both divine and mortal. Deception through metamorphosis was often featured in these stories, as here with the seduction of Leda.

Leda was the virtuous wife of Tyndareus of Sparta. When Jupiter desired her, he assumed the seemingly innocent disguise of a swan. Their liaison resulted in a most unusual birth. Leda's children are prominently featured in Greek mythology, particularly in connection with the Trojan War.

Sources

Homer, *Odyssey* 11.298–304 • Homeric Hymn 33 to the Dioscuri • Pindar, *Nemean Ode* 10.49–90 • Euripides, *Helen* 17–21, 214–17, 257–59, 1144–46 • Apollodorus, *Bibliotheca* (The Library) 3.10.6–7, 3.11.2 • Theocritus, *Idyll* 22 • Vergil, *Aeneid* 6. 121–22 • Ovid, *Fasti* 5. 715–20 • Lucian, *Dialogues of the Gods* 26

fidēlis, -e - *faithful, loyal*
coniūnx, -ugis, m./f. - *partner in marriage, husband*
cycnus, -ī, m. - *swan*
accēdō, -ere, -cessī, -cessum - *to come near, approach*
mansuētus, -a, -um - *tame*
trahō, -ere, trāxī, tractum - *to attract, fascinate, charm*

5 permulceō, -ēre, -mulsī, -mulsum - *to caress, stroke, pet*
penna, -ae, f. - *wing*
tegō, -ere, tēxī, tēctum - *to cover, hide*
coniungō, -ere, -iūnxī, -iūnctum (+ cum + abl.) - *to join together, mate*
ōvum, -ī, n. - *egg*
prōdūcō, -ere, -dūxī, -ductum - *to produce, bring forth*
geminus, -ī, m. - *twin*
sēmideus, -a, -um - *half-divine, demigod*
Pollux, ūcis, m. - *Pollux*
Castor, ōris, m. - *Castor*

10 bellissimus, -a, -um - *most beautiful*
tumultus, -ūs, m. - *disturbance, tumult*

ēveniō, -īre, -vēnī, -ventum - *to come out, happen*
anteā (adv.) - *before, formerly*
pulchritūdō, -dinis, f. - *beauty*
Athēnās: with names of cities the preposition *ad* may be omitted
abripiō, -ere, -ripuī, -reptum - *to remove by force, carry away, abduct*

15 nē ... abriperet: subjunctive clause of fearing (see Wheelock, Ch. 40), translate *that ... would abduct*
aliquī, -qua, -quod (indefinite adj.) - *some*
procus, -ī, m. - *suitor*
prōmittō, -ere, -mīsī, -missum - *to promise*
ēligō, -ligere, -lēgī, -lectum - *to choose, select*
cēterī, -ae, -a - *the other*

20 Menelāus, -ī, m. - *Menelaus*
Agamemnōn, -onis, m. - *Agamemnon*
Atreus, -ī, m. - *Atreus*, king of Mycenae, a city in Argos on the Peloponnesus in Greece
Mycēnae, -ārum, f. pl. - *Mycenae*

Grammar and Comprehension Questions

1) To whom does *sē* refer?
2) What qualities of the swan enticed Leda?
3) What was unusual about the children's birth?
4) What case is *illā eādem nocte*? What is its function?
5) What tense is *abripuerat*?
6) What tense is *accipiam*?
7) What gender is *hoc*? To what does it refer?
8) What did all the suitors of Helen promise?

Iuppiter Lēdam, rēgīnam Spartae, cupiēbat, sed fidēlis Lēda
coniugem Tyndareum amābat. Lēda sōla prope flūmen ambulābat.
Iuppiter igitur **sē** in bellum cycnum mūtāvit, ad quem Lēda tum
accessit. Lēda ā bellō mansuētōque cycnō tracta est et cycnum
permulcēre coepit. Mox cycnus eam pennīs tēxit et cum eā coniūnxit. 5
Illā eādem nocte Tyndareus etiam Lēdam amāvit. Sīc Lēda ē duōbus
patribus gravida facta est. Quod ūnus pater, Iuppiter, erat cycnus,
Lēda duo ōva prōdūxit. In quōque ōvō erant geminī, puer puellaque.
Ex ūnō ōvō, cuius Iuppiter erat pater, sēmideī līberī nātī sunt: Helena
et Pollux.[1] Ex alterō ōvō, cuius Tyndareus erat pater, mortālēs līberī 10
nātī sunt: Clytaemnestra[2] et Castor.

Fīlia Helena erat bellissima omnium fēminārum. Multī virī
igitur eī nūbere cupiēbant et magnus tumultus ēvēnit. Anteā Thēseus
iuvenālem Helenam propter pulchritūdinem Athēnās **abripuerat**,
sed tum geminī frātrēs Helenae eam ab Athēnīs ēripuerant. Nunc 15
pater Tyndareus timēbat nē aliquī procus iterum Helenam ā Spartā
abriperet. Dēnique cōnsilium cēpit: necesse erat omnēs procōs hoc
prōmittere: "**Accipiam** marītum quem Helena ēliget. Sī ūllus procus
Helenam abripiet, cum cēterīs procīs bellum contrā hunc geram."
Postquam omnēs **hoc** prōmīsērant, Helena Menelāum, fīlium Atreī, 20
rēgis Mycēnārum ēlēgit. Itaque post mortem Tyndareī Menelāus rēx
Spartae factus est. Etiam Agamemnōn, senior fīlius Atreī, sorōrī
Helenae, Clytaemnestrae, nūpsit. Itaque Clytaemnestra rēgīna
Mycēnārum facta est.

Discussion Questions

1) Why did Theseus abduct Helen? Have you heard about another abduction of Helen?
2) In addition to being sisters, what is the other relationship between Helen and Clytaemnestra?

---

1 The Greek name for Pollux was Polydeuces.
2 Her name has a number of variant spellings: Clytemnestra, Clytaemestra, etc.

25 **Dioscurī, -ōrum, m.** - *the Dioscuri, in Greek means "children of Zeus," the Greek Jupiter*

Argonautae, -ārum, m. pl. - *the Argonauts, heroes who sailed in the Argo with Jason*

pugil, -gilis, m. - *boxer, pugilist*

eques, -itis, m. - *horseman*

posterius (adv.) - *later*

quīdam, quaedam, quiddam or **quoddam** (indefinite pron. and adj.) - *a certain one, thing; some*

pugna, -ae, f. - *fight, battle*

trīstis, -e - *sad, sorrowful; grim*

vultus, -ūs, m. - *face; appearance, look, aspect*

30 **reddō, -ere, -didī, -ditum** - *to give back, return*

commūnicō (1) - *to share*

invicem (adv.) - *in turn, alternately*

īnferī, -ōrum, m. pl. - *the dead*

35 **appāreō, -ēre, -uī, -itum** - *to appear, be visibile*

custōdiō, -īre, -īvī or **-iī, -ītum** - *to keep safe, protect*

Grammar and Comprehension Questions

1) What were the special skills of Castor and Pollux?
2) What does Pollux beg from Jupiter?
3) What form is *permitte*?
4) What word do you understand with this *ūnum*?

Frātrēs Castor Polluxque "Dioscurī" appellābantur et cum Argonautīs 25
nāvigāvērunt. Ambō erant clārī pugilēs equitēsque et mīlitēs validī
fortēsque. Posterius tamen in quādam pugnā Castor interfectus est.
Pollux nimis dolēbat et mortem frātris tolerāre nōn poterat. Pollux
igitur trīstī vultū Iovem rogāvit: "**Permitte** mihi etiam ā vītā discēdere
aut frātrem meum ad mē redde." Quoniam Pollux erat immortālis, 30
Iuppiter mortem eī nōn permīsit, sed immortālitātem cum frātre
commūnicāre permīsit. Ut poēta Homērus nūntiat, geminī invicem
vīvunt: dum alter vīvit, alter mortuus est. Sed ut poēta Pindarus
nuntiat, frātrēs ūnum diem in Olympō, tum **ūnum** in īnferīs ūnā agunt.
Nunc frātrēs in caelō appārent et nautās custōdiunt. 35

Discussion Questions

1) What is the difference between Homer's and Pindar's accounts of how Castor and Pollux share immortality?
2) Where can we see the Gemini today?
3) Where can you find a very famous temple of Castor and Pollux? Investigate the historical event that this temple commemorates.

Cultural Influences

Art: The image of Leda and the swan has been most popular with artists. The most famous depictions are paintings by Leonardo da Vinci, but the theme has been treated by a veritable catalogue of the world's great painters including Michelangelo, Antonio da Correggio, Tintoretto, Veronese, Peter Paul Rubens, Nicholas Poussin, François Boucher, Gustave Moreau, Paul Cezanne, Henri Fantin-Latour, Man Ray, Mark Rothko, Henri Matisse, Paul Wunderlich, Roy Lichtenstein, and Salvador Dalí. Sculptors such as Filarete (relief on bronze door of St. Peter's, Rome, 1433–45) and Brancusi have also depicted the liaison. Artists have also been attracted to the Dioscuri, such as Horatio Greenough's bas relief of Castor and Pollux (1847–51) and Giorgio de Chirico's many treatments of the Dioscuri (1930ff.).

Literature: Edmund Spenser in *The Fairie Queen* 3.11.32 (1590) includes Leda in a tapestry of "Cupid's Wars;" Goethe, *Faust* Part 2, 2. 6903–20; poems entitled "Leda" by Rainer Maria Rilke (1908), H. D. (1919), Aldous Huxley (1920), William Butler Yeats (1924), Robert Graves (1938), Archibald MacLeish "The Rape of the Swan" (1948), and George Santayana "The Dioscuri" (1902).

Music: Opera/ballet "Castor and Pollux" by Jean-Philippe Rameau (1737). Ballets entitled "Leda" by Frederick Ashton with Marie Rambert (1928) and by Maurice Béjart (1979). Operas on the Dioscuri theme by numerous composers; ballets on the Dioscuri by Anthony Tudor (1934) and Frederick Ashton (1938).

Chapter Nineteen

The Prelude to War I: The Wedding of Peleus and Thetis; The Judgment of Paris

There was an ancient prophecy that the son born to Thetis, a Nereid or sea-goddess, would be stronger than his father. The son's strength could then lead to the overthrow of his father. This was the secret that Prometheus had kept until his release from Jupiter (see Chapter 5). Therefore no god wanted to sleep with Thetis. Zeus decreed that Thetis should marry a mortal, Peleus, king of Phthia in northern Greece. Thetis had the ability to metamorphose into any creature or natural force. Since she was unwilling to marry a mortal, Peleus had to capture and hold her during many transformations before she returned to her original shape and agreed to marry him. Both humans and gods attended their wedding, held on Mt. Peleion. The son of Peleus and Thetis was indeed greater than his father: he was Achilles, the great Greek hero whom Homer features in the *Iliad*. The passage here describes an episode during the wedding, which led directly to the Judgment of Paris and the Trojan War. In the description of the Judgment of Paris, the language echoes Ovid in *Heroides* 16.

Sources

Pindar, *Isthmian Ode* 8.26–60 • Herodotus, *Histories* 2.112–20 • Euripides, *Iphigenia in Aulis* 700–15, 1036–79; *Trojan Women* 920–32, 969–1072; *Andromache* 274–308; *Helen* 22–30 • Apollonius of Rhodes, *Argonautica* 4.796–809 • Catullus 64.19–51, 267–383 • Ovid, *Heroides* 16.57–88 (Paris to Helen); *Metamorphoses* 11.217–66 • Lucian, *Dialogues of the Sea Gods* 7; *Dialogues of the Gods* 20 (a satirical account of the Judgment)

Eris, -idis, f. - *Eris;* Greek goddess of discord, dissension, strife

nūptiae, -ārum, f. pl. - *wedding, marriage ceremony*

mālum, -ī, n. - *apple*

dēiciō, -ere, -iēcī, -iectum - *to throw down*

pulcherrimus, -a, -um - *most beautiful*

5 quisque, quaeque, quidque - *each one, each*

postulō (1) - *to demand, ask*

sapienter (adv.) - *wisely*

10 Paris, -idis, m. - *Paris;* prince of Troy; also called Alexander

ēligō, -ere, -lēgī, -lectum - *to choose, select*

aestimō (1) - *to value, assess, appreciate*

Īda, -ae, f. - *Ida,* mountain near Troy in Phrygia (now western Turkey)

mūrus, -ī, m. - *wall*

tēctum, -ī, n. - *building; roof*

prospiciō, -ere, -spexī, -spectum - *to look over, survey*

cōnstō -āre, -stitī - *to stand up, stand erect, stand*

digitus, -ī, m. - *finger*

virga, -ae, f. - *staff, wand*

simul (adv.) - *at the same time*

Pallas, -adis, f. - *Pallas;* another name for Minerva

grāmen, -minis, n. - *grass*

tener, -era, -erum - *soft, tender, delicate*

impōnō, -ere, -posuī, -positum - *to place on*

obstipēscō, -ere, -stipuī - *to be struck dumb, be stunned, amazed*

gelidus, -a, -um - *icy, chill, cold*

coma, -ae, f. - *hair*

15 ērigō, -ere, -rēxī, -rēctum - *to raise up, make stand up*

pōnō, -ere, posuī, positum - *to place, put;* here, *place aside*

inquit: *he says*

Grammar and Comprehension Questions

1) What tense, person, number, and voice is *invītābantur*?
2) Who is not invited to the wedding? Why?
3) What case and number is *hospitēs*?
4) What is the antecedent of *quō*?
5) What case is *pulcherrimae*? What is its function?
6) Why does Jupiter refuse to judge the contest?
7) Why is Mercury's name placed at the end of the sentence?
8) What is Mercury holding? What is its function?

Omnēs deī deaeque nisi Eris, dea discordiae, ad nūptiās **invītābantur**.
Nam quis Discordiam ad nūptiās invītat? Tamen īrāta Discordia inter
hospitēs subitō advēnit. In mediōs **hospitēs** aureum mālum dēiēcit
in **quō** īnscrībēbātur: "dōnum **pulcherrimae**." Sed quis deārum erat
pulcherrima? Trēs deae erant: Iūnō, Minerva, et Venus. Quaeque sibi   5
hoc mālum postulābat, sed ūna sōla esse pulcherrima poterat. Sīc
deae inter sē disputābant; dēnique Iovem rogāvērunt: "Cui hoc mālum
est? Quis nostrum est pulcherrima?" Sed Iuppiter inter uxōrem et duās
fīliās iūdicāre sapienter recūsāvit. Tum Iuppiter mortālem iūdicem,
Paridem, ēlēgit. Nam Paris, fīlius rēgis Trōiae, pulchritūdinem bene   10
aestimābat. Paris dē monte Īdā mūrōs tēctaque Trōiae prōspiciēbat,
cum subitō ante oculōs cōnstitit **Mercurius**. In digitīs deī aurea virga
fuit. Simul trēs deae, Venus et cum Pallade Iūnō, in grāminibus
tenerōs pedēs imposuērunt. Paris obstipuit, gelidusque horror comās
ērēxit. Tamen Mercurius "Pōne metum" inquit.   15

Discussion Questions

1) Do you know of another myth in which a human must master a meta-
morphosing god? Who is the human? Who is the god?
2) Peleus must physically conquer Thetis before she agrees to marriage.
What symbolic significance do you find in this fact?
3) Can you think of other myths in which a son presents a threat to his
father?
4) What is the relationship of Minerva and Venus to Jupiter? To each
other?

arbiter, -trī, m. - *judge, arbiter*
certāmen, -minis, n. - *contest, argument*
sistō, -ere, stitī, statum - *to stop, stay, end*
bonum animum habēre: *to take courage*
notō (1) - *to note, observe*
bellissimus, -a, -um - *most beautiful*

dignus, -a, -um (+ inf.) - *worthy (to)*
sollicitō (1) - *to tempt*
rēgnum, ī, n. - *kingdom*
inquit: here, *she said*
tālis, -e - *such*
reveniō, -īre, -vēnī, -ventum - *to come back, return*

Grammar and Comprehension Questions

1) What case is *hīs verbīs?* What is its function?
2) What case is *iūdicium?* Is it subject or object?
3) What tense, person, and number is *eris?*
4) Do the goddesses compete fairly?
5) How does Venus flatter Paris?
6) What case and function is *mālum?*

Judgment of Paris

"Arbiter es formae; certāmen deārum siste." **His verbīs** Paris bonum animum habuit nec timuit quamque deam oculīs notāre. Omnēs deae erant bellissimae et dignae vincere. Omnēs autem vincere cupiēbant. **Iūdicium** Paridis igitur ingentibus dōnīs sollicitāre temptāvērunt. Coniūnx Iovis magna rēgna in Asiā prōmīsit; Minerva victōriam in omnibus bellīs prōmīsit. Venus autem rīsit et pulchritūdinem Paridis laudāvit. "Tū ipse" inquit "es pulcher; vērus arbiter igitur formae **eris**. Tālis iūdex sōlus est dignus pulcherrimam mortālem fēminam habēre. Helenam, fīliam Lēdae, tibi dabō." Pulchritūdō Veneris et dōnum Paridī placēbant. Ergō aureum **mālum** Venerī dedit. Laeta dea cum mālō in manū ad caelum revēnit.

Discussion Questions

1) Why might Paris fear to look directly at the goddesses? Do you know of any myths that involve viewing a god directly?
2) Where was Paris when the gods appeared to him? What was he doing?
3) What would we call the gifts that the three goddesses offer?
4) Is there a fundamental difference between what Juno offers and what Minerva offers?

Cultural Influences

Art: The marriage of Peleus and Thetis and the Judgment of Paris have been especially popular subjects for artists. There are literally hundreds of examples of the Judgment of Paris; Peter Paul Rubens alone produced five versions! The following is a very brief, representative selection.

The Marriage of Peleus and Thetis: paintings or drawings entitled "The Wedding of Peleus and Thetis" by Cornelis van Haarlem (before 1593); Joachim Wtewael, five versions beginning in 1602; Peter Paul Rubens (1636); Joseph Turner, painting "The Goddess of Discord Choosing the Apple of Contention in the Garden of the Hesperides" (1806); Angelica Kauffmann, painting "Peleus and Thetis" in which Peleus approaches Thetis asleep in a cave (1807).

The Judgment of Paris: paintings by Lucas Cranach (1530); Jacopo Tintoretto (1543–44); Joachim Wtewael (three paintings beginning in 1602); Claude Lorrain "Landscape with the Judgment of Paris" (1633); Antoine Watteau (c. 1718–20); François Boucher (1754) including several in which Cupid offers the prize apple to Venus; Angelica Kauffmann (1781); William Blake (c. 1811); Paul Cézanne (1860–61); Henri Fantin-Latour (1863–65); Pierre Auguste Renoir (1908) as well as statuettes and bas-reliefs of Venus; John Singer Sargent in mural series at the Museum of Fine Arts, Boston (1916–21); Giorgio de Chirico (1946); Salvador Dalí (1950); Pablo Picasso (1951).

Literature: Pierre de Ronsard in *Livret de folastries* uses the Judgment of Paris to symbolize the triumph of lust over wisdom and virtue; William Congreve, masque "The Judgment of Paris," libretto for musical piece (1701); also masque by Thomas Augustine Arne (1740). Lord Alfred Tennyson treats the Judgment of Paris in his epyllion "Oenone," lines 77–202 (1832). Milan Kundera, story "The Golden Apple of Eternal Desire," in *Smesné lásky [Laughable Loves]* (1963); Robert Graves, poem *"The Judgment of Paris"* in *Man Does, Woman Is* (1964).

Music and Ballet: Jean-Philippe Rameau, cantata *"Thétis"* in which Neptune and Jupiter court her (1718). George Frederic Handel, serenata "Il Parnasso in festa," or "Apollo and the Muses Celebrating the Nuptials of Thetis and Peleus" (1734). Ballet by Marius Petipa "Les adventures de Pélée" with music by Léon Minkus (1876). Frederick Ashton ballet with music by Lennox Berkeley *The Judgment of Paris* (1938); Antony Tudor, satiric ballet *The Judgment of Paris* with music by Kurt Weill (1938).

Chapter Twenty

THE PRELUDE TO WAR II: THE ABDUCTION OF HELEN AND THE SACRIFICE OF IPHIGENIA

After Paris gave Venus the apple of victory, he was eager to claim his prize: Helen, the most beautiful woman in the world. There was one problem, however: she was already married to Menelaus, king of Sparta. This fact did not deter Paris and, with the guidance of the goddess, he sailed to Sparta. What happened there is still a matter of controversy: was Helen abducted, or did she go willingly with Paris? Did she go to Troy at all? Rather than simplify the myth and its many variants, this chapter includes multiple endings and explanations. You, the reader, can choose the ending that seems most appropriate to you.

When Helen left for Troy, Menelaus reminded Helen's former suitors of the pact they had made. The Greeks were honor-bound to make war against Troy and retrieve Helen. The assembly of the army led to the second episode described here: the sacrifice of Iphigenia. Similar to the abduction of Helen, the story is controversial and shows the richness and complexity of mythology. Interestingly, Homer does not seem to know this story, since it is never referred to in either the *Iliad* or the *Odyssey*. The passage here will examine the questions: who demanded Iphigenia's sacrifice and why? Was she actually sacrificed? Once again this passage provides multiple explanations and endings from which you can choose.

The language in the passage describing the abduction of Helen is modeled on Ovid's *Heroides* 16 and 17. In the sacrifice of Iphigenia the language is based upon Lucretius.

SOURCES

For the abduction of Helen: • Homer, *Iliad* 3. 153–65 • Stesichorus of Himera, *Palinode to Helen* • Euripides, *Helen* 31–46, 676ff; *Trojan Women* 914–1059, *Iphigenia in Tauris* • Lucian, *Dialogues of the Dead* 5 (Menippus and Hermes), 27 (Aeacus and Protesilaus) • Ovid, *Heroides* 16 (Paris to Helen); 17 (Helen to Paris)

For the sacrifice of Iphigenia: • Euripides, *Iphigenia in Aulis* • Lucretius, *De rerum natura* 1.84–103 • Vergil, *Aeneid* 2.116–19 • Ovid, *Metamorphoses* 12.1–38, 13.182–95

secundus, -a, -um - *favorable, following*
celeriter (adv.) - *swiftly, quickly*
Mycēnae, -ārum, f. pl. - *Mycenae, city ruled by Menelaus in Greece*
Mycēnās: with names of cities the preposition *ad* may be omitted
Paris, -ridis, m. - *Paris;* prince of Troy; also called Alexander
salūtō (1) - *to welcome, greet*
hospitium, -ī, n. - *hospitality,* the Greek *xenia*, which required guests and hosts to respect each other's property and family members
custōdiō, -īre, -īvī or **-iī, -ītum** - *to protect, preserve, oversee*
5 **prōtinus** (adv.) - *immediately, at once*
obstipēscō, -ere, -stipuī - *to be struck dumb, be stunned, amazed*
ārdēscō, -ere - *to catch fire, become excited or inflamed*
similis, -e (+ dat.) - *like*
iūdicium -iī, n. - *judgment, decision; trial*

patefaciō, -ere, -fēcī, -factum - *to make open, disclose, reveal*
vulnus, -neris, n. - *wound*
flamma, -ae, f. - *flame*
certē (adv.) - *certainly*
iuvenis, -e - *young, youthful*
an (conj.) - *or,* introducing the second part of a double question
pudor, -dōris, m. - *shame, modesty*
lābēs, -is, f. *-stain, disgrace*
10 **volēbat:** *was wanting, wanted*
fūrtīvus, -a, -um - *secret*
indignus, -a, -um - *unworthy*
māior, -ōris (adj.) - *greater*
Trōiam: with names of cities the preposition *ad* may be omitted
largus, -a, -um - *plentiful, bountiful, lavish*
dīvitiae, -ārum, f. pl. - *riches, wealth*
dēliciae, -ārum, f. pl. - *delights, comforts*
decet (+ dat.): *is fitting, right*

Grammar and Comprehension Questions

1) How did Venus help Paris get his prize?
2) What is the antecedent of *quibus?* What case is it and what is its grammatical function?
3) What case and number is *mōrēs?* What is its function?
4) Why did Menelaus trust Paris in his house?
5) Who is the subject of *vīdit* and *obstipuit?*
6) What tense is *patefēcerat?*
7) What about Helen so entranced Paris?
8) What case is *Paridī* and what is its function?
9) What does Paris say to Helen about the worth of her husband?

Venus, laeta victōriā, ventōs secundōs excitāvit **quibus** Paris
celeriter ad Graeciam nāvigāvit. Mox Mycēnās advēnit. Ibi rēx
Menelāus Paridem hospitem salūtāvit, quod **mōrēs** hospitiī quōs
Iuppiter custōdit accipiēbat. Dum Paris cum Menelāō cēnat,
Helenam prīmum **vīdit** et prōtinus **obstipuit**. Animus novās cūrās   5
sēnsit et ignibus amōris ārdēscēbat. Nam Helena habēbat similēs
vultūs eīs quōs Venus ipsa in iūdiciō **patefēcerat**. Etiamne Helena
vulnus flammamque amōris sēnsit? Hic hospes certē et iuvenis et
pulcher erat. An rēgīna pudōrem fāmamque sine lābe et fīdem uxōris
tenēre volēbat? **Paridī** autem Helena quoque amōre ārdēscere   10
vidēbātur. Itaque Paris fūrtīvās litterās ad rēgīnam mīsit, in quibus
scrīpsit: "Vir tuus indignus tē tenet. Pulchritūdō tua māiōrem fāmam
habēre dēbet. Mēcum Trōiam nāvigā! Ibi largīs dīvitiīs novīsque
dēliciīs luxuriāre poteris, ut tibi decet."

Discussion Questions

1) Examine Helen's feelings when she saw Paris.
2) Paris lures Helen to Troy with promises of wealth. Was Mycenae or Menelaus' palace poor?

15 opus, operis, n. - *need*
opus erat (+ dat. + infinitive): *there was a need for* (dat.)*, it was necessary for* (dat.) *to*
Crēta, -ae, f. - *Crete, an island in the Mediterranean south of Greece*
fīdenter (adv.) - *confidently, with assurance*
fīdō, -ere, fīsus sum (+ abl.) (semi-deponent verb; see Wheelock, Ch. 34) - *to trust (in), rely (on)*
rēgia, -ae, f. - *palace*
Hermionē, -ēs, f. - *Hermione*
absēns, -sentis (adj.) - *absent, away*
mandō (1) (+ dat. + infinitive) - *to entrust to, delegate to*

20 neglegēns, -gentis (adj.) - *negligent, careless*
peccō (1) - *to do wrong, offend*
iugālis, -e - *of marriage, matrimonial, nuptial*
nūpta, -ae, f. - *bride*
modo (adv.) - *only*
cubiculum, -ī, n. - *bedroom*
usquam (adv.) - *anywhere*
aerārium, -iī, n. - *treasury*
25 libenter (adv.) - *willingly, freely*
clāmor, -mōris, m. - *shout, cry*
fortasse (adv.) - *perhaps*
noceō, -ēre, -uī, -itum (+ dat.) - *to do harm to, harm, injure*
dēnūntiō (1) - *to threaten*

Grammar and Comprehension Questions

1) With whom does *absēns* agree?
2) What case, gender, and number is *vēra*? What is its function in the clause?
3) What case is *ūnō diē*? What is its function?
4) What voice is *invenīrī*?
5) What else did Paris take to Troy with Helen?
6) What do the servants speculate has happened to Helen? What alternate explanations of her behavior do they consider?

Mox opus erat Menelāō ad Crētam nāvigāre. Fīdenter nāvigābat, 15
quod mōribus hospitiī fīdēbat. Paridem in rēgiā cum Helenā et fīliā
Hermione relīquit.

Etiam **absēns** Helenae administrāre rēgnum et agere cūram
nōbilis hospitis mandāvit. Paris Helenae dīxit: "Marītus ipse
neglegēns cōnsilium nostrum adiuvat. Nōn peccābimus sī ea nunc 20
facimus quae hōra iugālis permittit. Nam nūpta mea mox eris, sī
modo Venus mihi **vēra** prōmīsit." **Ūnō diē** servī Helenam in cubiculō
invenīre nōn poterant. Nec Paris usquam **invenīrī** poterat. Dēnique
servī aerārium vacuum quoque invēnērunt. Servī sē rogant:
"Helenane rapta est? An libenter cum Paride fūgit? Sī rapta est, 25
cūr nēmō clāmōrem eius audīvit? An fortasse Paris Hermionī nocēre
dēnūntiāverat, sī Helena cum sē fugere recūsāvit."

Paris leads Helen to Troy

nōnnūllī, -ae, -a - *not none, a few, some*
scrīptor, -tōris, m. - *writer, author*
explicātiō, -tiōnis, f. - *explanation, account*
30 imāgō, -ginis, m. - *image, likeness*
fingō, -ere, finxī, finctum - *to fashion, make, create*
Aegyptus, -ī, f. - *Egypt*
quō (adv.) - *where, in which place*
35 īnfidēlis, -e - *unfaithful*
maximē (adv.) - *very greatly*
Ulixēs, -is, m. - *Ulysses,* the Greek Odysseus
Ithaca, -ae, f. - *Ithaca,* island off the western coast of Greece
poscō, -ere, poposcī - *to demand, require*
reddō, -ere, -didī, -ditum - *to give back, return*

fūrtum, -ī, n. - *theft; stolen good*
cōnsentiō, -īre, -sēnsī, -sēnsum - *to consent, agree*
inexpugnābilis, -e - *impregnable, unassailable*
40 voluntās, -tātis, f. - *will, wish*
raptam esse: from *rapiō, -ere,* perfect passive infinitive in indirect statement (see Wheelock, Ch. 25), *had been stolen*
procus, -ī, m. - *suitor*
convocō (1) - *to call together, convene, summon*
Agamemnōn, -onis, m. - *Agamemnon*
exercitus, -ūs, m. - *army*
plūrimus, -a, -um - *very many, the most*
imperō (1) (+ dat.) - *to command, be in control of*

Grammar and Comprehension Questions

1) What tense, person, number, and voice is *victa est?* Who is its subject?
2) Where do other authors say Helen spent the duration of the war? Why?
3) What does Menelaus demand from the Trojans? How do the Trojans react?
4) What case is *voluntāte?* What is its function?
5) What tense, person, number, and voice is *factus est?* With whom does it agree?

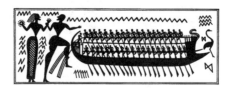

Paris and Helen board a ship

Nōnnūllī scrīptōrēs[1] aliam explicātiōnem habēbant: Helena numquam Trōiam nāvigāvit. Iūnō erat īrāta quod in iūdiciō Paridis **victa est**. Dea igitur falsam imāginem Helenae finxit, quam Paridī dedit. Iūnō tum Mercurium iussit Helenam ad Aegyptum dūcere, quō per tōtum bellum remanēbat. Sīc Trōiānī fatālem bellum prō imāgine pugnāvērunt.

Menelāus ā Crētā revēnit et domum sine uxōre invēnit. Miser eam, quamquam īnfidēlem, maximē vidēre dēsīderābat. Cum Ulixe, rēge Ithacae, Troiam nāvigāvit et poposcit: "Nisi Helenam aerāriumque ad mē reddētis, magnum bellum contrā Trōiam geram." Multī Trōiānī fūrta reddere cupiēbant, sed rēx Priamus nōn cōnsēnsit, quod Trōia inexpugnābilis in bellō ante fuerat. Priam etiam crēdidit Helenam **voluntāte** deōrum raptam esse. Menelāus ad Graeciam revēnit et procōs, quī prōmīserant Helenam raptam ēripere, convocāvit. Agamemnōn, senior frāter, dux exercitūs **factus est**, quod plūrimīs cōpiīs imperābat.

Discussion Questions

1) Examine the concept and practices of guest-friendship. Was Menelaus simply gullible and too trusting in leaving Paris in Mycenae?
2) Do you believe Helen went willingly with Paris or was abducted by him?

---

1 Stesichorus of Himera, Herodotus, Eurpides in *Electra*

Aulis, -lidis, f. - *Aulis, a seaport town on the eastern coast of Greece*
Aulidem: with names of cities the preposition *ad* may be omitted
custōs, -tōdis, m. - *guardian, protector*
45 **offendō, -ere, -dī, -fēnsum** - *to offend against, wrong*
inhibeō, -ēre, -uī, -itum - *to hold back, restrain*
tam (adv. used to intensify adjectives and adverbs) - *so*
magnē (adv.) - *greatly*
inrītō (1) - *to move to anger, provoke*
cerva, -ae, f. - *hind, female deer*
cāsus, -ūs, m. - *accident, chance*
aquila, -ae, f. - *eagle*
lepus, -poris, m. - *hare;* here clearly a female animal despite the gender of the noun
similiter (adv.) - *similarly*
50 **arbor, -boris, f.** - *tree*
octō (indeclinable adj.) - *eight*
pullus, -ī, m. - *nestling, young bird*
dēvorō (1) - *to devour*
Calchās, -chantis, m. - *Calchas, Greek seer*
Agamemnona: accusative singular masculine
maximus, -a, -um - *greatest*

nātū: ablative singular masculine, *by birth;* with **maximam**, *eldest*
flō (1) - *to blow*
classis, -is, f. - *fleet, naval force*
tālis, -e - *such*
55 **numquam** (adv.) - *never*
potius (adv.) - *rather*
Ulixēs, -is, m. - *Ulysses, the Greek Odysseus*
dehonestō (1) - *to discredit, disgrace*
postulātiō, -tiōnis, f. - *demand*
premō, -ere, pressī, pressum - *to press, press hard*
60 **timidus, -a, -um** - *cowardly*
Achillēs, -is, m. - *Achilles*
iter, itineris, n. - *journey*
domī - *at home*
65 **nūptiae, -ārum, f. pl.** - *wedding, marriage ceremony*
adsum, -esse, -fuī, -futūrus (+ dat.) - *to be present at*
gerēns: feminine singular nominative present active participle (see Wheelock, Ch. 23), *wearing,* taking **vestēs** as its direct object
vestis, -is, f. - *clothing, dress, attire*
nūpta, -ae, f. - *bride*
āra, -ae, f. - *altar*
minister, -trī, m. - *priest's attendant, assistant*

Grammar and Comprehension Questions

1) What are the principal parts of the verb from which *mīsit* comes?
2) What familiar English word is derived from *classis*? Can you see the connection?
3) What would have happened if Agamemnon had refused Diana's demands?
4) Why would Ulysses want to invent or tamper with the prophecy given to Agamemnon?
5) Why is *verbīs* in the dative case?
6) What is the antecedent of *quibus*?
7) How is Iphigenia dressed?

Exercitus Aulidem convēnit. Sed tum dea Diāna, custōs animālium, maximē offēnsa est et ventōs inhibēbat. Exercitus igitur Trōiam 45 nāvigāre nōn poterat.

Quid tam magnē deam inrītāvit? Ut nōnnūllī dīcunt[2], Agamemnōn cervam sacram Diānae cāsū interfēcit. Ut aliī nuntiant[3], Iuppiter ōmen **mīsit** in quō duae aquilae gravidum leporem interfēcērunt. Similiter aliī nūntiant[4] ōmen in quō serpēns arborem ascendit et octō pullōs cum 50 mātre dēvorāvit. Tum vātēs Calchās nūntiāvit: "Dea Diāna poenās poscit. Necesse est Agamemnona fīliam maximam nātū, Iphigenīam, sacrificāre. Sine hōc sacrificiō ventī nōn flābunt nec **classis** nāvigāre poterit."

Nōnnūllī[5] autem aliam explicātiōnem dant: deī tāle sacrificium numquam poposcērunt; potius aliī, praesertim Ulixēs, Agamemnona 55 dehonestāre et sē ducēs facere cupiēbant. Sed exercitus **verbīs** Calchantis crēdidit.

Prīmum Agamemnōn postulātiōne deae terrēbātur et fīliam sacrificāre recūsābat. Sed frāter Menelāus et Ulixēs premēbant et Agamemnona timidum vocābant. Dēnique Agamemnōn litterās ad 60 Iphigenīam scrīpsit, in **quibus** eam Aulidem advocāvit. Scrīpsit: "Magnus Achillēs Trōiam nōn nāvigābit nisi prīmum Iphigenīae nūbet." Iphigenīa igitur sē fēlīcem crēdidit et laeta Aulidem iter fēcit. Māter Clytaemnestra, quamquam iūssa erat manēre dōmī, tamen vēnit, quod nūptiīs adesse cupiēbat. Innocēns Iphigenīa, gerēns vestēs nūptae, ad 65 āram ambulāvit. Ibi ante āram pater Agamemnōn et ministrī stābant.

Discussion Questions

1) What might the omen of the eagle and the hare indicate? What might the omen of the snake and nestlings indicate?
2) Can Agamemnon be held responsible for omens sent to him by Jupiter?
3) What did the Greeks usually believe regarding human sacrifice?
4) Why do you think Clytaemnestra was told to stay in Mycenae?

---

2 Sophocles in the tragedy *Electra*
3 Aeschylus in the tragedy *Agamemnon*
4 Ovid in *Metamorphoses*
5 Euripides in the tragedy *Iphigenia in Aulis*

fleō, -ēre, -ēvī, -ētum - *to weep, lament*
cēlō (1) - *to hide, conceal*
aspectus, -ūs, m. - *appearance, sight*
lacrima, -ae, f. - *tear*
effundō, -ere, -fūdī, -fūsum - *to pour out, forth*
adhaereō, -ēre, -haesī, -haesum (+ dat.) - *to cling to*

70 prōsum, -desse, -fuī (+ dat.) - *to help, be of use, do good*
quod prīma rēgem patrem vocāverat: the clause acts as the subject of **poterat**
trepidus, -a, -um - *filled with alarm, terrified*
dēducta est: Lucretius uses this verb ironically, since this verb was also used for a bride being led to her spouse's house as part of the wedding ceremony.
velut (adv.) - *just as, like*
hostia, -ae, f. - *sacrificial victim*
mactō (1) - *to slaughter sacrificially*
ut ... darētur: imperfect tense subjunctive mood passive voice in a purpose clause (see Wheelock, Ch. 28 and 29): translate *so that ... would be given*
aliter (adv.) - *otherwise, differently*

dēscrībō, -ere, -scrīpsī, -scrīptum - *to describe, write about*
75 tandem (adv.) - *at last, finally*
fortiter (adv.) - *bravely*
cōnstō, -āre, -stitī - *to decide, determine*
nōlēbant: *they were unwilling*
āvertō, -ere, -vertī, -versum - *to turn away, avert*
80 Eurīpidēs, -is, m. - *Euripides*
mīrus, -a, -um - *wonderful, surprising, extraordinary*
effundentem: accusative singular feminine present active participle (see Wheelock, Ch. 23), *pouring forth,* modifying **cervam;** the participle takes a direct object **sanguinem**
exsolvō, -ere, -uī, -ūtum - *to set free, release*
Taurī, -ōrum, m. pl. - *the Tauri,* a people living on the north shore of the Black Sea
sacerdōs, -dōtis, m. - *priestess*
permīsit: takes the dative case
85
ut ... redūcerētur: imperfect subjunctive passive in a purpose clause: translate *so that ... would be brought back.*

Grammar and Comprehension Questions

1) What does Iphigenia see that makes her become fearful?
2) What case is *metū*? What is its function?
3) What gender, number, and case is *multī*? What word do you understand with it?

Sed cūr pater flēbat? Cūr ministrī gladiōs cēlābant? Cūr cīvēs aspectū Iphigenīae lacrimās effundēbant? Iphigenīa mūta **metū** terram petēbat et genibus patris adhaerēbat. Lacrimīs vītam petēbat, sed miserae puellae prōdesse nōn poterat, quod prīma rēgem patrem 70
vocāverat. Trepida manibus virōrum sublāta est et ad ārās dēducta est. Tum velut hostia mactāta est ut fēlix exitus classī darētur.

Poēta Eurīpidēs autem rem aliter dēscrīpsit. Clytaemnestra Iphigenīaque terribile cōnsilium invēnērunt; Achillēs etiam Iphigenīam dēfendere prōmīsit. Tandem Iphigenīa fortiter cōnstitit 75
vītam suam prō patriā dare et ad āram libenter ambulāvit. Māter Clytaemnestra autem Agamemnona interficere iūrāvit quod pater fīliam mactāverat.

Multī horribile sacrificium spectāre nōlēbant et oculōs āvertēbant. Poēta Eurīpidēs in aliā tragoediā mīrum ēventum nūntiat. Ultimō 80
mōmentō aliī in ārā nōn Iphigenīam sed cervam sanguinem effundentem vīdērunt. Dea Diāna Iphigenīam exsolvit et ad Taurōs portāvit, quō sacerdōs deae facta est.

Post sacrificium Iphigenīae dea ventīs flāre permīsit. Classis mīlle nāvibus Trōiam celeriter nāvigāvit. Magnum bellum inter 85
Graeciam Trōiamque incēpit ut ūna mulier redūcerētur.

Discussion Questions

1) Which version of the sacrifice do you believe?
2) Do you know of a biblical story comparable to the sacrifice of Iphigenia? Who are the participants? What happens?
3) Do you know if Clytaemnestra fulfills her vow to punish Agamemnon? Where can you read about this story?

Cultural Influences

These two inter-related stories have inspired myriad works in multiple media. Only a brief sample is included below.

Art: paintings by Benozzo Gozzoli (1421–97), *The Rape of Helen* (early work); Fra Angelico, *The Rape of Helen by Paris* (c. 1450); *The Rape of Helen* in several versions by Jacopo Tintoretto (1580–85); Luca Giordano, several (1666–86); Giovanni Battista Tiepolo (c. 1755–60); Gustave Moreau (c. 1852); Angelica Kauffmann, five paintings on the Paris and Helen theme (1774ff); Jacques-Louis David *(The Loves of) Paris and Helen* (1788). Honoré Daumier, comic lithograph *The Abduction of Helen* (1842). Vincenzo de Rossi sculptural group *Paris and Helen* (1587). Paintings entitled *Sacrifice of Iphigenia* by Niccolo Giolfino (1555), Jan Steen (1671), Giovanni Battista Tiepolo, four versions (c. 1720–25), Mark Rothko (1942). Plaque *The Sacrifice of Iphigenia* by Josiah Wedgwood (c. 1795). New Yorker cartoon by Handelsman; *The Judgment of Paris*.

Ballet: Jean Coralli, *Helene et Paris* (1800); Isadora Duncan, *Iphigenia in Aulis* (1905).

Film: *Helen of Troy*, directed by Robert Wise (1956); *Iphigenia*, directed by Michael Cacoyannis (1977); *Troy*, directed by Wolfgang Petersen (2004).

Literature: Dante in *Inferno* 5.64–65 places Helen among the lustful (c. 1307–14); in *Paradiso* 5.68–72 Dante recalls Iphigenia's sacrifice (c. 1321); Giovanni Boccaccio, *De Helena, Menelai regis coniuge* in *De mulieribus claris* (1361–75); Lady Jane Lumley, *The Tragedie of Euripides Called Iphigeneia*, drama after Euripides and Erasmus (1558); Lope de Vega drama *Entremés del robo de Elená* (Intermezzo of the Rape of Helen) (1635); Jean Racine, *Iphigénie en Aulide*, tragedy (1674); Friedrich von Schiller verse drama *Iphigenie in Aulis* (1790); Alfred Lord Tennyson, poem "A Dream of Fair Women" 84–122 features Helen and Iphigenia (1831–32).

Music: many operas, including Domenico Scarlatti, *Iphigenia in Aulide* (1713) and Camille Saint-Saëns, *Hélene* (1904); Christoph Willibald Gluck music for ballet *Iphigénie* (1765) and operas *Paride ed Elena* (1770) and *Iphigénie in Aulide* (1774). Luigi Cherubini opera-ballet *Iphigenia in Aulide* (1782). Johann Nepomuk Hummel music for ballet *Helene und Paris* (1807). Peter Schickele (a.k.a. P. D. Q. Bach), satirical cantata *Iphigenia in Brooklyn* (c. 1970s).

Agamemnon Sacrifices His Daughter, Iphigenia

Genealogical Charts

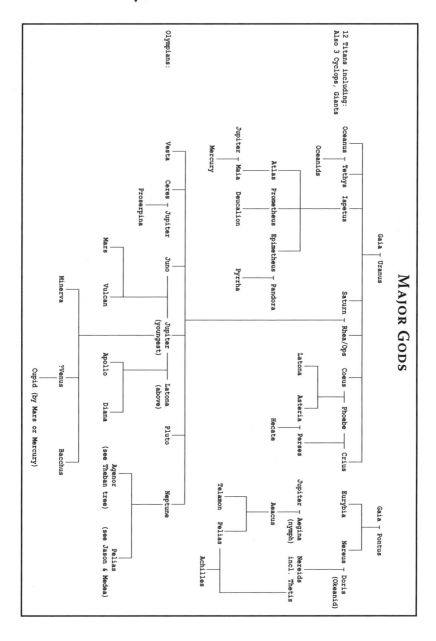

The Theban Tree
Underlined names are those that appear in the text.

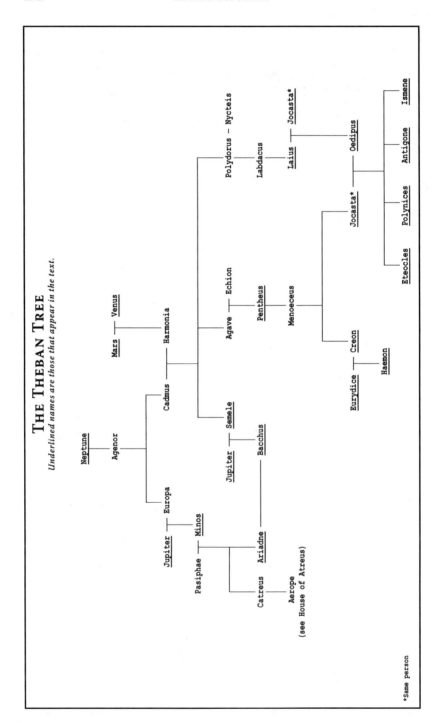

*Same person

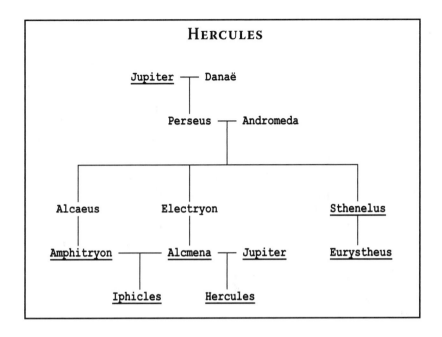

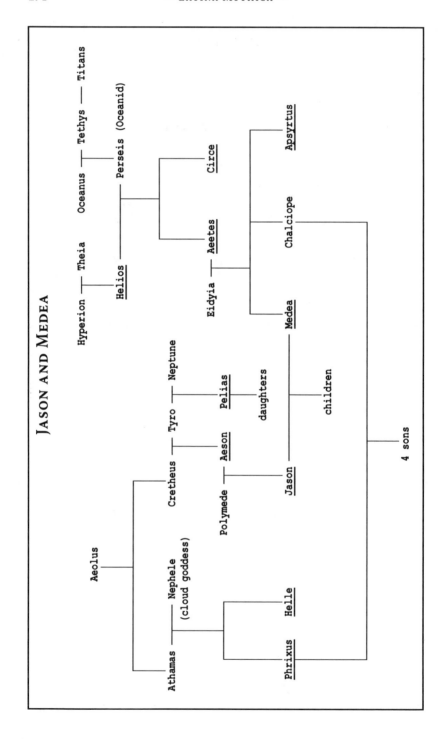

Genealogical Charts

House of Atreus

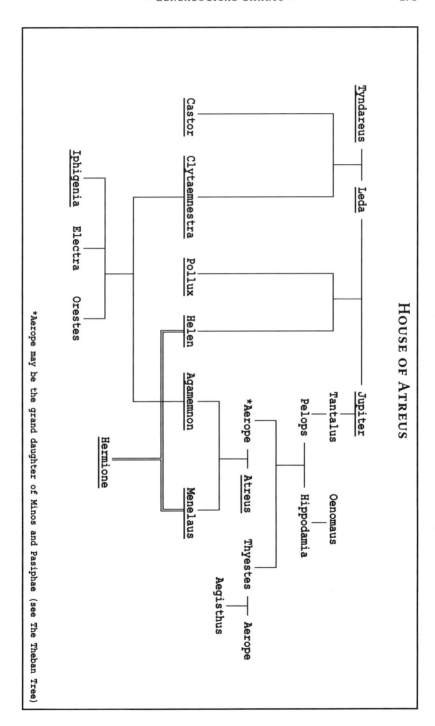

*Aerope may be the granddaughter of Minos and Pasiphae (see The Theban Tree)

Ancient Sources Cited

Aeschylus: Greek (525–456 BC): tragedies on mythological themes: *Prometheus Bound, Seven Against Thebes*.

Apollodorus: Greek (c. 140 BC): *Bibliotheca* or *The Library*. This compendium of mythology surviving under his name may be a later compilation of the first or second century AD.

Apollonius of Rhodes: Greek (c. 295–215 BC): *Argonautica*, a four-book epic describing the adventures of Jason and his Argonauts in retrieving the golden fleece.

Bacchylides: Greek (end of sixth to middle of fifth century BC): lyric poet; epicinian (victory) odes.

Bible, *Genesis*: Hebrew (material compiled beginning in tenth century BC): first book of the Old Testament of the Bible with the story of creation, man's fall from grace, Cain and Abel, Noah, Abraham's sacrifice of Isaac.

Catullus, Gaius Valerius: Roman (c. 84–c. 54 BC): lyric and elegiac poet. Mostly writes personal and political poetry, but in his longer poems includes mythological material.

Diodorus Siculus: Greek (fl. c. 60–30 BC): *Bibliotheca Historica*, or *Universal History*; an uncritical retelling of universal ancient history including legendary material. Incomplete.

Epic of Gilgamesh: Sumerian (c. 700 BC): recounts story of a great flood from about 2700 BC

Euripides: Greek (c. 485–406 BC): tragedies on mythological themes: *Andromache, Bacchae, Helen, Hippolytus, Iphigenia in Aulis, Iphigenia among the Taurians, Medea, The Suppliants, Phoenician Women, Trojan Women*.

Herodotus: Greek (c. 490–c. 425 BC): considered the father of history; *Histories*, which depict the wars between the Greeks and Persians, contains much other information and stories of interest both historically and anthropologically.

Hesiod: Greek (c. 700 BC): epic poet writing in the Boeotian or catalogue-style of epic: *Shield of Heracles, Theogony, Works and Days*.

Homer: Greek (probably eighth century BC): epic poet of the *Iliad*, recounting the wrath of Achilles in the last year of the Trojan War, and of the *Odyssey*, telling of Odysseus' (Ulysses') ten-year journey home from the war.

Homeric Hymns: part of epic cycle composed between the eighth and sixth centuries BC. Each hymn is dedicated to a particular god or goddess. Their content varies from simple praise of the divinity to detailed mythological narrative.

Horace (Quintus Horatius Flaccus): Roman (65–8 BC): poet who became Rome's poet laureate; close friend of his patron Maecenas and of the emperor Augustus; lyric *Odes*.

Lucian: wrote in Greek but was born in Samosata, now in eastern Turkey (c. 115–c. 180 AD); prolific lecturer, essayist, and satirist writing in the style of Plato: *Dialogues of the Dead, Dialogues of the Gods, Dialogues of the Sea Gods*.

Lucretius (Titus Lucreitus Carus): Latin (c. 94–c. 54 BC): *De rerum natura*, a didactic epic promoting Epicurean philosophy, a materialist philosophy that denies the traditional depiction of the Graeco-Roman gods; includes an extremely poignant passage on the sacrifice of Iphigenia as an example of the evils religion has caused.

Ovid (Publius Ovidius Naso): Roman (43 BC–17 AD): prolific poet whose epic *Metamorphoses* has been for centuries a primary guide to Greek mythology; also in the mythological tradition is the *Heroides*, letters from legendary women to their lovers that concludes with some paired letters; *Fasti*, an account of the first six months of the Roman calendar including legendary information.

Pindar: Greek (518–after 446 BC): lyric poetry in epinician odes that often compare the feats of the victor with famous mythological heroes of the past: *Isthmian Odes, Nemean Odes, Olympian Odes, Pythian Odes*.

Plato: Greek (427–347 BC): Philosopher and pupil of Socrates; includes references to mythology in some of his prose works; here *Protagoras*.

Plautus, Titus Maccius: Roman (c. 250–184 BC): one of the earliest Roman authors; writer of comedy in the Greek New Comedy style; *Amphitryon* is rare because it has a mythological setting.

Plutarch: Greek (c. 46–c. 120 AD): biographer, historian, and philosopher; his *Parallel Lives* has provided moral instruction by example for generations.

Seneca, Lucius Annaeus the Younger: Roman (c. 4 BC–65 AD): Stoic philosopher, orator, senator; he also composed nine tragedies on mythological themes; here *Medea, Oedipus, The Phoenician Maidens*.

Sophocles: Greek (c. 496–406/5 BC): tragedies on mythological themes: *Antigone, Oedipus at Colonus, Oedipus the King, Women of Trachis.*

Stesichorus of Himera, Sicily: Greek (first half of sixth century BC): Palinode to Helen in which he retracts his former criticism of her and claims she never went to Troy.

Theocritus: Greek (first half of third century BC): Hellenistic poet from Sicily who wrote pastoral *Idylls* which often included mythological themes.

Vergil (Publius Vergilius Maro): Roman (70–19 BC): great Roman poet, friend of Horace, his patron Maecenas, and the emperor Augustus; his didactic farming epic, *Georgics,* includes some mythological material, particularly the story of Orpheus and Eurydice; his epic *Aeneid* recounts the foundation story of Rome after the fall of Troy.

Bibliography

REFERENCE BOOKS ON MYTHOLOGY

Bulfinch, Thomas. *Myths of Greece and Rome.* Introduction, Joseph Campbell. Compiler, Brian Holme. New York: Penguin, 1979.

Grant, Michael. *Myths of the Greeks and Romans.* London: Weidenfeld and Nicolson, 1962; New York: Mentor Books, 1964.

Graves, Robert. *The Greek Myths.* 2 vols. Baltimore: Penguin Books. 1993.

Grimal, Pierre. *The Concise Dictionary of Classical Mythology.* Oxford: Basil Blackwell, 1990.

Hamilton, Edith. *Mythology.* New York: Mentor Books, 1942.

Howatson, M. C. *The Oxford Companion to Classical Literature.* Oxford: Oxford University Press, 1989.

James, Vanessa. *The Genealogy of Greek Mythology.* New York: Gotham Books; Penguin, 2003.

Mayerson, Philip. *Classical Mythology in Literature, Art, and Music.* Glenview, IL: Scott, Foresman and Co., 1971.

Morford, Mark P. O. and Lenardon, Robert J. *Classical Mythology.* Seventh Edition. New York: Oxford University Press, 2003.

Parada, Carlos. *Genealogical Guide to Greek Mythology. Studies in Mediterranean Archaeology,* vol. 107. Coronet Books, 1993.

Rose, H. J. *A Handbook of Greek Mythology.* New York: Dutton & Co., 1959.

Tripp, Edward. *The Meridian Handbook of Classical Mythology.* New York: New American Library, 1970.

Other sources

Gilder, Eric, and June Port. *The Dictionary of Composers and their Music.* New York: Paddington Press, 1978.

Hartigan, Karelisa V. *Muse on Madison Avenue: Classical Mythology in Contemporary Advertising.* Frankfurt: Peter Lang, 2002.

Winkler, M. Martin, ed. *Classics and Cinema.* Bucknell Review 35.1. Cranbury, NJ.: Associated University Presses, 1991.

Poduska, Donald M., "Classical Myth in Music: A Selective List." *Classical World* 92.3 (1999), 195–276.

Reid, Jane Davidson. *The Oxford Guide to Classical Mythology in the Arts 1300–1990s.* 2 vols. New York: Oxford University Press, 1993.

Solomon, Jon. *The Ancient World in the Cinema.* New Haven: Yale University Press, 2001.

Solomon, Jon, "In the Wake of *Cleopatra*: The Ancient World in the Cinema since 1963." *Classical World* 91.2 (1996), 113–40.

Internet resources

Greek mythology link by Carlos Parada, author of *Genealogical Guide to Greek Mythology* (1993); contains essays, images of mythological motifs, and maps: http://homepage.mac.com/cparada/GML/

The Perseus Project with texts, maps, art works, site plans, and other resources: http://www.perseus.tufts.edu/

Website for Morford and Lenardon text (above): http://www.classicalmythology.org

Maecenas site with pictures of mainly Roman sites and objects: http://wings.buffalo.edu/AandL/Maecenas

Museum of Fine Arts, Boston has many classical objects, especially vases depicting classical mythology. One can search by mythological figure: http://www.mfa.org

Many other museums also have excellent web sites on which one can find ancient art and art influenced by the ancient myths. Most museum websites have search features so that one can look for works by individual artists and/or on certain mythological characters.

See in particular:

The British Museum, London: http://thebritishmuseum.ac.uk/compass

The Metropolitan Museum of Art, New York: http://metmuseum.org

The National Gallery, London: http://nationalgallery.org.uk/

One can find other museum sites quite easily by searching for the museum name on http://www.google.com. You may want to search the website of the museum closest to you to see what classical and classically influenced works they own. The websites may also include works that are not regularly on display in the galleries.

Vocabulary

A

ā or ab (prep. + abl.) - *from, away from*
abdūcō, -ere, dūxī, -ductum - *to lead away, take away*
absēns, -sentis - *absent*
absum, -esse, -fuī, -futūrus - *to be absent, away*
accēdō, -ere, -cessī, -cessum - *to come near, approach*
accelerō (1) - *to hasten, speed up, accelerate*
accidō, -ere, -cidī - *to happen, occur*
accipiō, -ere, -cēpī, -ceptum - *to take, receive, accept*
ācer, ācris, ācre - *sharp, keen, severe*
acerbus, -a, -um - *harsh, bitter, grievous*
Achillēs, -is, m. - *Achilles, son of Peleus and Thetis, Greek hero of the Trojan war*
ad (prep. + acc.) - *to, up to, towards*
addō, -ere, -didī, -ditum - *to add*
adiuvō (1) - *to help, aid; please*
administrō (1) - *to manage, administrate*
admittō, -ere, -mīsī, -missum - *to admit, receive, let in*
adolēscō, -ere, -olēvī - *to become mature, grow up*
adoptō (1) - *to adopt*
adōrō (1) - *to worship*
adsum, -esse, -fuī, -futūrus - *to be present*
adsūmō, -ere, -sumpsī, -sumptum - *to take to oneself, assume*
adulēscēns, -centis, m./f. - *young man, young woman*
adveniō, -īre, -vēnī, -ventum - *to arrive at, come to*
advocō (1) - *to call to, summon*
aedificō (1) - *to build, construct*
aemula, -ae, f. - *rival (in love)*
Aenēas, -ae, m. - *Aeneas, son of Venus and Anchises, Trojan prince and hero who becomes founder of Roman culture*
aēneus, -a, -um - *of bronze*
aequus, -a, -um - *even, calm*
āēr, āeris, m. - *air*
aestās, -tātis, f. - *summer*
aetās, -tātis, f. - *age, time*
aeternus, -a, -um - *eternal*
aetherius, -a, -um - *ethereal, heavenly*
aevum -ī, n. - *age*
ager, agrī, m. - *field, farm*
agitō (1) - *to drive, ride*
agnōscō, -ere, -nōvī, -nitum - *to recognize*
agō, -ere, ēgī, actum - *to drive, lead, do, act; conduct; pass, spend*
  grātiās agere (+ dat.) - *to thank someone, to give thanks to*
aliquis, aliquid (pronoun) - *someone, something*
alius, alia, aliud - *other, another, different*
  aliī . . . aliī: *some, others*
alō, -ere, -uī, altum - *to nourish, support, sustain, increase, cherish*

alter, -era, -erum - *the other (of two), second*
altus, -a, -um - *high, deep*
ambō, ambae, ambō - *both*
ambulō (1) - *to walk*
amīcitia, -ae, f. - *friendship*
amīca, -ae, f. - *(female) friend*
amīcus, -ī, m. - *(male) friend*
amīcus, -a, -um - *friendly*
amittō, -ere, -mīsī, -missum - *to lose, let go*
amō (1) - *to love*
amor, -ōris, m. - *love*
amputō (1) - *to cut off, amputate*
anima, -ae, f. - *soul, spirit*
animal, -mālis, n. - *animal, living creature*
animus, -ī, m. - *soul, spirit, mind*
  animī, -ōrum, m. pl. - *high spirits, pride, courage*
annus, -ī, m. - *year*
ante (prep. + acc.) - *before, in front of;* (adv.) *before, previously*
aperiō, -īre, -uī, -tum - *to open*
appellō (1) - *to call, name*
Apollō, -linis, m. - *Apollo, god of the sun, music, prophecy*
aqua, -ae, f. - *water*
aquila, -ae, f. - *eagle*
āra, -ae, f. - *altar*
arbor, -boris, f. - *tree*
arcānum, -ī, n. - *secret*
arcus, -ūs, m. - *bow*
ardeō, -ēre, arsī - *to catch fire, burn, be burnt to death*
argenteus, -a, -um - *of silver*
arma -ōrum, n. pl. - *arms, weapons*
arō (1) - *to plow*
ars, artis, f. - *art, skill*

artificium, -iī, n. - *handicraft, craftsmanship*
ascendō, -ere, -dī, -sum - *to go up, ascend*
Asia, -ae, f. - *Asia*
at (conj.) - *but* (more emotional than *sed*)
atque or ac (conj.) - *and, and also, and even*
Athēnae, -ārum, f. pl. - *the city of Athens*
Athēnaeus, -ī, m. - *Athenian*
audax, -dācis - *daring, bold*
audeō, -ēre, ausus sum - *to dare*
audiō, -īre, -īvī, -ītum - *to hear, listen to*
aura, -ae, f. - *breath, air, wind*
aureus, -a, -um - *golden*
auris, -is, f. - *ear*
aut (conj.) - *or*
aut... aut: *either... or*
autem (postpositive conj.) - *however, moreover*
auxilium, -iī, n. - *aid, help*
avis, -is, f. - *bird*

B

Baccha, -ae, f. - *Bacchante, female devotee of Bacchus*
Bacchus, -ī, m. - *Bacchus, god of wine, the Greek Dionysus*
barbarus, -a, -um - *non-Greek, foreign, barbarian*
beātus, -a, -um - *happy, blessed, fortunate*
bellum, -ī, n. - *war*
bellus, -a, -um - *pretty, handsome, charming*
bene (adv. of **bonus**) - *well, satisfactorily, quite*
beneficium, -iī, n. - *kindness, favor, benefit*

bestia, -ae, f. - *wild animal, beast*
bonus, -a, -um - *good, kind*
bōs, bovis, m. - *bull, ox, cow;* plural, *cattle*
brācchium, -iī, n. - *arm*
brevis, -e - *short, small, brief*
breviter (adv.) - *in short, briefly*

C

cadō, -ere, cecidī, cāsūrus - *to fall*
caecus, -a, -um - *blind*
caelum, -ī, n. - *sky, heaven*
callidus, -a, -um - *clever, crafty*
calor, -lōris, m. - *warmth, heat*
candidus, -a, -um - *bright, white*
capiō, -ere, cēpī, captum - *to take, capture, seize, get*
caput, -pitis, n. - *head; leader; beginning*
carcer, -ceris, m. - *jail, prison*
careō, -ēre, caruī, caritūrus (+ abl. of separation) - *to lack, want; be free from*
carpō, -ere, -psī, -ptum - *to pluck at*
cārus, -a, -um - *dear*
cavus, -a, -um - *hollow*
cēdō, -ere, cessī, cessum - *to yield, withdraw, go*
celer, -eris, -ere - *swift, quick, rapid*
celeriter (adv.) - *swiftly, quickly*
celeritās, -tātis, f. - *speed, swiftness*
cēlō - *to hide, conceal*
cēnō (1) - *to dine, eat*
centum (indeclinable adj.) - *hundred*
Cerēs, -eris, f. - *Ceres,* goddess of agriculture, the Greek Demeter
certē (adv.) - *certainly*
certus, -a, -um - *certain, sure, reliable*
cessō (1) - *to stop, cease*
cēterī, -ae, -a - *the others, rest*

cibus, -ī, m. - *food*
cito (adv.) - *quickly*
cīvis, -is, m./f. - *citizen*
clam (adv.) - *secretly, under cover*
clāmō (1) - *to call, shout, cry aloud*
clāmor, -mōris, m. - *shout, cry*
clārus, -a, -um - *clear, bright; famous*
claudō, -ere, clausī, clausum - *to shut, close*
claudus, -a, -um - *lame*
coepī, coepisse, coeptum (defective verb; in perfect only) - *began*
cōgitō (1) - *to think, conisder*
cognōscō, -ere, -nōvī, -nitum - *to get to know, recognize;* in perfect, *to know*
cōgō, -ere, coēgī, coāctum - *to compel*
collis, -is, m. - *hill, hill-top*
colō, -ere, coluī, cultum - *to worship*
comitō (1) - *to accompany, attend*
committō, -ere, -mīsī, -missum - *to entrust, commit*
concēdō, -ere, -cessī, -cessum - *to grant, admit, concede*
conditor, -ōris, m. - *founder*
coniūnx, -ugis, m./f. - *partner in marriage, consort, husband, wife*
cōnsentiō, -īre, -sēnsī, -sēnsum - *to agree*
cōnsilium, -iī, n. - *plan, advice*
cōnspiciō, -ere, -spexī, -spectum - *to spot, catch sight of*
cōnstāns, -tantis - *standing firm, resolute*
cōnsul, -sulis, m. - *consul*
contentus, -a, -um - *content, satisfied*
contrā (prep. + acc.) - *against*
conveniō, -īre, -vēnī, -ventum - *to assemble, meet, convene*
copia, -ae, f. - *abundance, supply*
copiae, -ārum, f. pl. - *supplies, troops, forces*

cōpiōsus, -a, -um - *abundant, plentiful*
coquō, -ere, coxī, coctum - *to cook*
cornū, -ūs, n. - *horn*
corōnātus, -a, -um - *crowned, wreathed*
corpus, -poris, n. - *body*
cōtīdiē (adv.) - *daily*
crēdō, -ere, -didī, -ditum (+ dat.) - *to believe, trust*
creō (1) - *to create*
crēscō, -ere, crēvī, crētum - *to come into existence, arise, grow, increase*
Crēta, -ae, f. - *Crete, an island in the Mediterranean*
cruciō (1) - *to torture, torment*
culpa, -ae, f. - *blame, responsibility, guilt*
culpō (1) - *to blame*
cultūra, -ae, f. - *agriculture*
cum (prep. + abl.) -*with*
cumba, -ae, f. - *small boat, skiff*
cupiditās, -tātis, f. - *desire, longing, passion*
cupiō, -ere, -īvī, -ītum - *to desire, wish, long for*
cūr (adv.) - *why*
cūra, -ae, f. - *care, concern, anxiety*
cūrō (1) - *to care for*
currō, -ere, cucurrī, cursum - *to run, rush, move quickly*
currus, -ūs, m. - *chariot*
custōs, -tōdis, m. - *guard*

D

damnō (1) (+ abl. of penalty) - *to condemn to*
dē (prep. + abl.) - *down from, down; concerning, about*
dea, -ae, f. - *goddess*
dēcernō, -ere, -crēvī, -crētum - *to decide, settle, decree*

dēclārō (1) - *to make known, announce, declare*
decus, -coris, n. - *honour, esteem, glory*
dēdūcō, -ere, -dūxī, -ductum - *to draw out; lead down*
dēfendō, -ere, -fendī, -fēnsum - *to defend, ward off, protect*
deinde (adv.) - *thereupon, next, then*
dēlectō (1) - *to delight, charm, please*
dēleō, -ēre, -ēvī, -ētum - *to destroy, obliterate*
dēmōnstrō (1) - *to point out, show, indicate, demonstrate*
dēnique (adv.) - *at last, finally*
dēns, dentis, m. - *tooth*
dēpōnō, -ere, -posuī, -positum - *to lay down, take down, get rid of*
dēscendō, -ere, -scendī, -scēnsum - *to descend*
dēsertus, -a, -um - *deserted, unpopulated*
dēsīderō (1) - *to desire, long for, miss*
dēsistō, -ere, -titī (+ abl.) - *to leave off, cease*
dēspērō (1) - *to despair, give up hope*
dēsum, -esse, -fuī, -futūrus - *to be missing, lacking*
deus, -ī, m. - *god*
dēvorō (1) - *to devour, consume*
dexter, -tra, -trum - *right, right-hand*
Diāna, -ae, f. - *Diana, goddess of the hunt, the moon, the Greek Artemis*
dīcō, -ere, dīxī, dictum - *to say, tell, speak; name, call*
difficilis, -e - *hard, difficult*
diēs, diēī, m. - *day*
dignus, -a, -um (+ abl.) - *worthy*
dīligō, -ere, -lēxī, -lectum - *to esteem, love, cherish*
dīluvium, -iī, n. *flood, deluge*
discēdō, -ere, -cēssī, -cēssum - *to go away, depart*

discō, -ere, didicī - *to learn*
discordia, -ae, f. - *discord, disagreement, strife*
disputō (1) - *to argue one's case, dispute*
dissideō, -sidēre, -sēdī - *to disagree, differ*
diū (adv.) - *long, for a long time*
diūtius (adv.) - *longer*
dīvidō, -ere, -vīsī, -vīsum - *to divide, distribute*
dīvīnus, -a, -um - *divine, sacred*
dīvitiae, -ārum, f. pl. - *riches, wealth*
dō, dare, dedī, datum - *to give*
doceō, -ēre, -uī, doctum - *to teach*
doctus, -a, -um - *learned, skilled*
doleō, -ēre, -uī, -itum - *to grieve, grieve for*
dolor, -lōris, m. - *grief, sorrow*
dolus, -ī, m. - *fraud, trick, deceit*
domus, -ūs, f. - *house, home;* **domī** - *at home;* **domum** - *(to) home;* **domō** - *from home*
dōnum, -ī, n. - *gift*
dormiō, -īre, -īvī, -ītum - *to sleep*
dubius, -a, -um - *doubtful, uncertain*
dūcō, -ere, dūxī, ductum - *to lead; consider, regard; prolong*
dulcis, -e - *sweet, pleasant*
dum (conj. with present indicative) - *while, as long as, at the same time that*
duo, duae, duo - *two*
dūrus, -a, -um - *hard, harsh, rough, hardy*
dux, ducis, m. - *leader, commander, general*

E

ē or **ex** (prep. + abl.) - *out of, from*
ecce (interjection) - *behold! look!*
ēdūcō, -ere, -dūxī, -ductum - *to lead out*
efficiō, -ere, -fēcī, -fectum - *to bring about, accomplish*
effugiō, -ere, -fūgī, -fugitūrus - *to escape, flee*
effundō, -ere, fūdī, -fūsum - *to pour out, forth*
ego, meī, mihi, mē, mē - *I, me*
ēligō, -ligere, -lēgī, -lectum - *to choose, select*
ēmittō, -ere, -mīsī, -missum - *to send out, release, let fly*
enim (postpositive conj.) - *for, in fact, truly*
equus, -ī, m. - *horse*
ērectus, -a, -um - *erect, upright*
ergō (adv.) - *therefore*
ēripiō, -ere, -ripuī, -reptum - *to snatch away*
errō (1) - *to wander, go astray, roam; be mistaken*
est - third person singular of **sum, esse**, *he/she/it is*
et (conj.) - *and, also*
etiam (adv.) - *also, even*
etiamnum or **etiamnunc** (adv.) - *even now, still, yet*
ēveniō, -īre, -vēnī, -ventum - *to come out, turn out, happen*
ēventus, -ūs, m. - *outcome, event, happening*
ēvolō (1) - *to fly out, forth*
ex (prep. + abl.) - *out of*
excēdō, -ere, -cēdī, -cēssum - *to go out, leave, depart*
excitō (1) - *to rouse, wake, stir up*
excūsō (1) - *to excuse, justify*
exerceō, -ēre, -uī, -itum - *to practice, exercise, perform*
exercitus, -ūs, m. - *army*
exhālō (1) - *to exhale, breathe out*
exitus, -ūs, m. - *exit, departure*

expello, -ere, -pulī, -pulsum - *to drive out, expel, banish*
expōnō, -ere, -posuī, -positum - *to expose, abandon*
exsecrātiō, -tiōnis, f. - *curse*
exsilium, -iī, n. - *exile, banishment*
exspectō (1) - *to look for, expect, await*
extrā (adv.) - *outside*

F

fābula, -ae, f. - *story, tale*
facilis, -e - *easy*
faciō, -ere, fēcī, factum - *to make, do, accomplish*
factum -ī, n. - *deed, act, achievement*
falsus, -a, -um - *false, deceptive*
familia, -ae, f. - *household, family*
fatālis, -e - *fatal, deadly*
fatīgō (1) - *to weary, tire, fatigue*
fātum, -ī, n. - *fate*
fēlix, -licis (adj.) - *lucky, fortunate, happy*
fēmina, -ae, f. - *female, woman*
fēriae, -ārum, f. pl. - *religious festival, holy day, holiday*
ferreus, -a, -um - *iron, of iron*
ferrum - ī, n. - *iron, sword*
ferus, -a, -um - *wild, uncivilized, fierce*
fervidus, -a, -um - *intensely hot, blazing*
fidēlis, -e - *faithful, loyal*
fidēs, -ēī, f. - *faith, trust, loyalty*
fīlia, -ae, f. - *daughter*
fīlius, -ī, m. - *son*
fīnis, -is, m. - *end, limit*
flamma, -ae, f. - *flame*
flāvus, -a, -um - *yellow, golden-colored*
flectō, -ere, flexī, flexum - *to bend, turn, change, alter*
flūmen, -minis, n. - *river*
fluō, -ere, flūxī, flūxum - *to flow*
focus, -ī, m. - *hearth*
fōrma, -ae, f. - *form, shape; beauty*
fōrmō (1) - *to form, shape, fashion*
fortasse (adv.) - *perhaps*
fortis, -e - *strong, brave*
fortūnātus, -a, -um - *lucky, fortunate, happy*
frāter, -tris, m. - *brother*
fraudō (1) - *to deceive, cheat*
frīgeō, -ēre - *to be cold*
frīgidus, -a, -um - *cold, frigid*
frūctus, -ūs, m. - *fruit, profit, benefit, enjoyment*
frūx, frūgis, f. - *fruit, crops*
fugiō, -ere, fūgī, fugitūrus - *to flee, hurry away; go into exile; avoid, shun*
fulgeō, -ēre, fulsī - *to shine, gleam*
fulmen, -minis, n. - *thunderbolt*
fūr, -ris, m. - *thief*

G

Gāia, -ae, f. - *Gaia, original goddess, mother earth*
galea, -ae, f. - *helmet*
gaudeō, -ēre, gāvīsus sum - *to rejoice, be glad*
geminus, -ī, m. - *twin*
gemō, -ere, -ui, -itum - *to groan*
generō (1) - *to produce, create*
gēns, gentis, f. - *clan, race, family, nation*
genū, -ūs, n. - *knee*
genus, -neris, n. - *class, kind, race*
gerō, -ere, gessī, gestum - *to carry, carry on, manage, conduct, wage*
gestō (1) - *to wear*
gladius, -iī, m. - *sword*
glōria, -ae, f. - *glory, fame*

Graecia, -ae, f. - *Greece*
Graecus, -a, -um - *Greek*
Graecī, -ōrum, m. pl. - *the Greeks*
grātia, -ae, f. - *gratitude*
grātiās agere: idiom, *to thank, give thanks*
grātus, -a, -um - *grateful*
gravidus, -a, -um - *pregnant*
gravis, -e - *heavy, weighty, serious, important, severe*
grex, gregis, m. - *herd, flock*
gubernō (1) - *to control, govern*

H

habeō, -ēre, -uī, -itum - *to have, hold*
habitō (1) - *to live, dwell*
hasta, -ae, f. - *spear*
hedera, -ae, f. - *ivy*
herba, -ae, f. - *grass, plants*
Herculēs, -is, m. - *Hercules, the Greek Heracles, son of Jupiter/Zeus and the mortal Alcmena*
herī (adv.) - *yesterday*
hērōs, hērōis, m. - *hero*
hic, haec, hoc - *this; the latter; he, she, it, they*
hīc (adv.) - *here*
hiems, -mis, f. - *winter*
hodiē (adv.) - *today*
homicīdium, -iī, n. - *murder*
homō, -minis, m. - *human being, man*
honor, -nōris, m. - *honor, esteem; public office*
hōra, -ae, f. *hour, time*
horrendus, -a, -um - *terrible, fearful, dreadful*
horribilis, e - *horrible, dreadful*
horror, -rōris, m. - *shivering, dread, horror*

hospes, -pitis, m. - *guest; host*
hostis, -is, m. - *enemy (of the state)*,
hostēs, -ium, m. pl. - *the enemy*
hūmānus, -a, -um - *human*
hūmānus, - ī, m. - *human being*

I

iaciō, -ere, iēcī, iactum - *to throw, hurl*
iactō (1) - *to throw, hurl*
iam (adv.) - *now, already, soon*
iānua, -ae, f. - *door, gate*
ibi (adv.) - *there*
īdem, eadem, idem - *the same*
igitur (postpositive conj.) - *therefore, consequently*
ignārus, -a, -um - *not knowing, ignorant*
ignis, -is, m. - *fire*
ignōrō (1) - *to have no knowledge of, be ignorant or unaware of*
ignōscō, -ere, -nōvī, -nōtum (+ dat.) - *to forgive, pardon*
ille, illa, illud - *that; the former; he, she, it, they*
illic (adv.) - *at that place, there*
imber, -bris, m. - *rain*
immortālis, -e - *immortal*
immortālitās, -tātis, f. - *immortality*
imperium, -iī, n. - *power to command, supreme power, authority*
impleō, -ēre, -lēvī, -lētum - *to fill up, complete*
impōnō, -ere, -posuī, -positum - *to place in*
in (prep. + acc.) - *into, toward; against;* (+ abl.) - *in, on*
incendium, -iī, n. - *fire*
incertus, -a, -um - *uncertain, in doubt*
incipiō, -ere, -cēpī, -ceptum - *to begin*
īnfāns, -fantis, m. - *infant, young child*

īnferī, -ōrum, m. pl. - *the dead*
īnfīnītus, -a, -um - *unlimited, infinite, endless*
ingenium, -iī, n. - *intelligence*
ingēns, ingentis - *huge*
inīquus, -a, -um - *unequal, unfair, unjust*
iniūria, -ae, f. - *injustice, injury, wrong*
innocēns, -entis - *not guilty, blameless, innocent*
innocuus, -a, -um - *innocent, blameless*
inquam, inquis, inquit (defective verb placed after one or more words of a quotation) - *I say, you say, he/she says*
īnsānus, -a, -um - *of unsound mind, mad, insane*
īnscrībō, -ere, -scrīpsī, -scrīptum - *to inscribe*
īnstituō, -ere, -stituī, -stitūtum - *to establish, set up, institute*
īnsula, -ae, f. - *island*
integer, -gra, -grum - *untouched, whole, unhurt*
intellegō, -ere, -lēxī, -lēctum - *to understand*
inter (prep. + acc.) - *between, among*
intereā (adv.) - *meanwhile*
interficiō, -ere, -fēcī, -fectum - *to kill*
intrō (1) - *to walk into, enter*
intus (adv.) - *within*
inveniō, -īre, -vēnī, -ventum - *to come upon, find, discover*
investīgō (1) - *to investigate, examine, search out*
invideō, -ēre, -vīdī, -vīsum (+ dat.) - *to be jealous of, feel ill will toward*
invītus, -a, -um - *unwilling*
invītō (1) - *to invite to come*
ipse, -a, -um - *himself, herself, itself, themselves*
īrātus, -a, -um - *angered, angry*

is, ea, id - *he, she, it; this* or *that person or thing*
iste, ista, istud - *that of yours, that; such*
itaque (adv.) - *and so, therefore*
iter, itineris, n. - *journey*
iterum (adv.) - *again, a second time*
iubeō, -ēre, iūssī, iūssum - *to order, command*
iūcundus, -a, -um - *pleasant, delightful, pleasing*
iūdex, -dicis, m. - *judge, juror*
iūdicium -iī, n. - *judgment, decision; trial*
iungō, -ere, iūnxī, iūnctum - *to join*
Iūnō, -nōnis, f. - *Juno,* wife of Jupiter, the Greek Hera
Iuppiter, Iovis, m. - *Jupiter, Jove,* the Greek Zeus
iūrō (1) - *to swear*
iūs, iūris, n. - *right, justice, law*
iūssum, -ī, n. - *order, command*
iūstitia, -ae, f. - *justice*
iuvenālis, -e - *young, youthful*
iuvenis, -is, m. - *a young man, youth*
iuvō (1) - *to help, aid, assist*

L

labor, -bōris, m. - *work, labor, toil*
labōrō (1) - *to labor, work, worry*
labyrinthus, -ī, m. - *labyrinth* (constructed by Daedalus in Crete)
lac, lactis, n. - *milk*
laetus, -a, -um - *happy, joyful*
lapis, -pidis, m. - *stone*
Latīnus, -a, -um - *Latin*
Lātōna, -ae, f. - *Latona,* mother of Apollo and Diana, the Greek Leto
laudō (1) - *to praise*
laus, laudis, f. - *praise, glory, fame*

legō, -ere, lēgī, lēctum - *to pick out, choose; read*
leō, leōnis, m. - *lion*
levis, -e - *light, easy, trivial*
levō (1) - *to raise, lift up*
lēx, lēgis, f. - *law*
libenter (adv.) - *willingly*
liber, -brī, m. - *book*
līberī, -ōrum, m. pl. - *(one's) children*
līberō (1) - *to free*
lībertās, -tātis, f. - *liberty*
ligō (1) - *to bind, fasten*
lingua, -ae, f. - *tongue; language*
literrae, -ārum, f. pl. - *letter, epistle*
lītus, -toris, n. - *shore*
locus, -ī, m. - *place*
    loca, -ōrum, n. pl. - *places, region*
    locī, -ōrum, m. pl. - *passages in literature*
longus, -a, -um - *long*
longē (adv.) - *far*
lūdō, -ere, lūsī, lūsum - *to play*
lūdus, -ī, m. - *game, sport*
lūgeō, -ēre, lūxī, lūctum - *to mourn, lament*
lūna, -ae, f. - *moon*
lupus, -ī, m. - *wolf*
lūx, lūcis, f. - *light, day*
luxuriō (1) - *to luxuriate in, indulge in*
lyra, -ae, f. - *lyre*, a stringed musical instrument

M

maestus, -a, -um - *sad, mournful, grief-stricken*
magis (adv.) - *more; rather*
magnus, -a, -um - *great*
maior, maius (adj.) - *greater in size, larger, older, more important*
malum, -ī, n. - *evil, misfortune*
mālum, -ī, n. - *apple*
mānō (1) - *to flow, drip*
manus, -ūs, f. - *hand; band*
mare, -is, n. - *sea*
marītus, -ī, m. - *husband*
Mars, Martis, m. - *Mars*, god of war, the Greek Ares
māter, -tris, f. - *mother*
māteria, -ae, f. - *material, matter*
mātrimōnium, -iī, n. - *marriage*
maximus, -a, -um - *greatest*
medicāmentum, -ī, n. - *drug*
medicīna, -ae, f. - *medicine*
medicus, -ī, m. - *doctor*
medius, -a, -um - *middle; the middle of*
mel, mellis, n. - *honey*
membrum, -ī, n. - *limb*
meminī, meminisse (defective verb; in perfect only) - *to remember*
memoria, -ae, f. - *memory, recollection*
mendīcus, -ī, m. - *beggar*
mēns, mentis, f. - *mind, thought, intention*
mēnsis, -is, m. - *month*
Mercurius, -ī, m. - *Mercury*, messenger god, the Greek Hermes
messis, -is, f. - *harvest*
metuō, -ere, -uī - *to fear, dread, reverence*
metus, -ūs, m. - *fear, anxiety, dread*
meus, -a, -um - *my*
mīles, mīlitis, m. - *soldier*
mīlia, -ium, n. pl. - *thousands*
mīlle (indeclinable. adj.) - *thousand*
Minerva, -ae, f. - *Minerva*, goddess of handicrafts, the Greek Athena

minimus, -a, -um - *smallest, youngest*
minor, minus (adj.) - *smaller in size, lesser, younger, inferior*
mīrus, -a, -um - *wonderful, surprising, extraordinary*
misceō, -ēre, -uī, mixtum - *to mix, stir up, disturb*
miser, -era, -erum - *wretched, miserable, unfortunate*
miseria, -ae, f. - *misery, unhappiness, wretchness, distress*
mittō, -ere, mīsī, missum - *to send, let go*
mixtus, -a, -um - *mixed*
modus, -ī, m. - *manner, way*
momentum, -ī, n. - *moment, instant*
moneō, -ēre, -uī, -itum - *to warn, advise*
monitiō, -tiōnis, f. - *admonition, warning*
mōns, montis, f. - *mountain*
mōnstrum, -ī, n. - *monster*
morbus, -ī, m. - *disease, sickness*
mors, mortis, f. - *death*
mortālis, -e - *mortal*
mortuus, -a, -um - *dead*
   mortuus, -ī, m. - *dead person, corpse*
mōs, mōris, m. - *habit, custom, manner*
moveō, -ēre, mōvī, mōtum - *to move; arouse, affect*
mox (adv.) - *soon*
multō (1) - *to punish*
multus, -a, -um - *much, many*
mundus, -ī, m. - *world, universe*
mūnus, -neris, n. - *service, function, duty; gift*
mūsica, -ae, f. - *music*
mūtō (1) - *to change, alter; exchange*
mūtus, -a, -um - *mute, speechless*
Mycēnae, -ārum, f. pl. - *Mycenae*, city ruled by Menelaus in Greece

N

nam (conj.) - *for*
narrō (1) - *to tell, narrate*
nāscor, -ī, nātus sum - (deponent verb; see Wheelock, Ch. 34), *to be born, spring forth, arise*
natō (1) - *to swim*
nātūra, -ae, f. - *nature*
nauta, -ae, m. - *sailor*
nāvigō (1) - *to sail, navigate*
nāvis, -is, f. - *boat, ship*
-ne (enclitic) - affixed to end of word to indicate a question
nē (conj.) - *not*
nec (conj.) - *and not, nor*
nec . . . nec: *neither . . . nor*
necesse (indeclinable adj.) - *necessary*
   necesse est: with accusative and infinitive, *it is necessary that [accusative] do [infinitive]*
necō - *to murder, kill*
neglegō, -ere, -lēxī, -lēctum - *to neglect, disregard*
negō (1) - *to deny, refuse*
nēmō, nūllīus, nēminī, nēminem, nūllō or nūllā, m./f. - *no one, nobody*
Neptūnus, -ī, m. - *Neptune*, god of the sea, the Greek Poseidon
neque (conj.) - *and not, no*
   neque . . . neque: *neither . . . nor*
nēquīquam (adv.) - *in vain, uselessly*
Nērēis, -idis, f. *a Nereid*, a sea-nymph
neuter, -tra, -trum - *not either, neither*
niger, -gra, -grum - *dark, black*
nihil (indeclinable adj.) - *nothing*
nimis or nimium - *too, too much, excessively*
nisi (conj.) - *if not, unless, except*
niveus, -a, -um - *snowy, white*

nix, nivis, f. - *snow*
nōbilis, -e - *noble, well-born*
noceō, -ēre, -uī, -itum (+ dat.) - *to do harm to, harm, injure*
nōmen, -minis, n. - *name*
nōn (adv.) - *not*
nōndum (adv.) - *not yet*
nōs, nostrum, nōbīs, nōs, nōbīs - *we, us*
noster, -tra, -trum - *our*
novus, -a, -um - *new, strange*
nox, noctis, f. -*night*
nūbēs, -is, f. - *cloud*
nūbō, -ere, nupsī, nuptum (+ dat.) - *to marry*
nūllus, -a, -um - *not any, no, none*
numquam (adv.) - *never*
nunc (adv.) - *now, at present*
nūntiō (1) - *to announce, report*
nūntius, -iī, m. - *messenger; message*
nuper (adv.) - *recently*
nūpta, -ae, f. - *bride*

O

obscūrus, -a, -um - *dark, dim, obscure*
obstinātus, -a, -um - *stubborn, obstinate, hardened*
oculus, -ī, m. - *eye*
octāvus, -a, -um - *eighth*
ōdī, ōdisse - (defective verb; in perfect only) *to hate*
officīna, -ae, f. - *workshop, place where something is made*
officium, -iī, n. - *duty, function*
ōlim (adv.) - *at that time, once, formerly; in the future*
Olympius, -a, -um - *Olympian*
Olympus, -ī, m. - *Olympus*, mountain in northern Greece sacred to the gods

ōmen, -minis, n. - *omen, augury*
omnis, -e - *all, every, each*
Ops, Opis, f. - *Ops*, the Greek Rhea, wife of Saturn, mother of Jupiter
optō (1) - *to desire, wish*
ōrāculum, -ī, n. - *oracle, prophecy*
orbis, -is, m. - *circle*
   orbis terrārum: *the world, earth*
orīgō, -ginis, f. - *origin, birth*
ōrō (1) - *to beg, beseech*
ōs, ōris, n. - *mouth, face*
os, ossis, n. - *bone*
ostium -iī, n. - *door, entrance*
ovis, -is, f. - *sheep*

P

pānis, -is, m. - *bread*
parēns, -rentis, m./f. - *parent*
pāreō, -ēre, -uī (+ dat.) - *to obey*
pariō, -ere, peperī, partum - *to produce, give birth to*
Paris, -ridis, m. - *Paris*; prince of Troy; also called Alexander
parō (1) - *to prepare, provide*
pars, partis, f. - *part, share*
parvus, -a, -um - *little, scanty*
patefaciō, -ere, -fēcī, -factum - *to make open, disclose, reveal*
pateō, -ēre, -uī - *to lie open, be open, be accessible, be evident*
pater, -tris, m. - *father*
patientia, -ae, f. - *suffering, patience, endurance*
patria, -ae, f. - *fatherland, native land, (one's) country*
pāx, pācis, f. - *peace*
pectus, -toris, n. - *chest*
pecūnia, -ae, f. - *money*

pellis, -is, f. - *hide, skin*
pellō, -ere, pepulī, pulsum - *to strike, push, drive*
pendeō, -ēre, pependī - *to hang suspended, hang*
penetrō (1) - *to pass through, penetrate, pierce*
penna, -ae, f. - *feather; wing*
per (prep. + acc.) - *through*
perdō, -ere, -didī, -ditum - *to destroy*
pereō, -īre, -iī, -itum - *to perish, die*
perfectus, -a, -um - *complete*
perficiō, -ere, -fēcī, -fectum - *to complete, accomplish*
perīculum, -ī, n. - *danger, risk*
permittō, -ere, -mīsī, -missum (+ dat.) - *to permit, allow*
persequor, -sequī, -secūtus sum - (deponent verb; see Wheelock, Ch. 34) *to follow constantly, pursue, chase*
persuādeō, -ēre, -suāsī, -suāsum (+ dat.) - *to persuade*
pertineō, -ēre, -uī - *to pertain, apply to*
pēs, pedis, m. - *foot*
pestis, -is, f. - *plague, pestilence, disease*
petō, -ere, -īvī, -ītum - *to seek, beg*
pictūra, -ae, f. - *painting, picture*
pietās, -tātis, f. - *dutifulness, respectfulness, piety*
piscis, -is, m. - *fish*
pius, -a, -um - *pious, faithful*
placeō, -ēre, -uī, -itum (+ dat.) - *to please*
placidus, -a, -um - *calm, tranquil, peaceful*
plēnus, -a, -um - *full, full of, abundant, generous*
plūrimus, -a, -um - *very many, very much*
Plūtō, -tōnis, m. - *Pluto*, ruler of the underworld, the Greek Hades
pōculum, -ī, n. - *drinking-vessel, cup, bowl*
pondus, -deris, n. - *weight, burden*
poena, -ae, f. - *penalty, punishment*
poenās dare: *to pay the penalty*
poēta, -ae, m. - *poet*
poētica, -ae, f. - *poetry*
pōnō, -ere, posuī, positum - *to place, put*
pontus, -ī, m. - *sea*
populus, -ī, m. - *the people, a people, nation*
porta, -ae, f. - *gate, entrance*
portō (1) - *to carry*
poscō, -ere, poposcī - *to demand, require*
possum, posse, potuī - *to be able, can*
post (prep. + acc.) - *after*
posteā (adv.) - *afterwards*
postquam (conj.) - *after*
postrēmō (adv.) - *finally*
postulō (1) - *to demand*
potēns, gen. **potentis** - *powerful, able, strong, mighty*
potestās, -tātis, f. - *power, influence*
praebeō, -ēre, -uī, -itum - *to offer, provide*
praesertim (adv.) - *especially*
praeter (prep. + acc.) - *besides, except*
praetereā (adv.) - *moreover, in addition*
prehendō, -ere, -hendī, -hēnsum - *to take hold of, grasp*
premō, -ere, pressī, pressum - *to press, press hard*
pretium, -iī, n. - *price, value*
prex, precis, f. - *prayer*
prīdem (adv.) - *long ago*
prīmō (adv.) - *at first, first*
prīmum (adv.) - *for the first time*
prīmus, -a, -um - *first*
principium, -iī, n. - *beginning*
prō (prep. + abl.) - *instead of, in place of; for, on behalf of*

procul (adv.) - *far, at a distance*
prōdō, -ere, -didī, -ditum - *to betray, forsake*
prōdūcō, -ere, -dūxī, -ductum - *to produce, bring forth*
proelium, -iī, n. - *battle*
prohibeō, -ēre, -uī, -itum - *to prevent, hinder, restrain, prohibit*
prōmittō, -ere, -mīsī, -missum - *to promise*
prōnūntiō (1) - *to make publicly known, declare*
prōnus, -a, -um - *prone, inclined forward*
prope (prep. + acc.) - *near*
propitius, -a, -um - *favorably inclined, well-disposed, propitious*
propter (prep. + acc.) - *on account of, because of*
Prōserpīna, -ae, f. - *Proserpina*, wife of Pluto, goddess of underworld, the Greek Persephone
prōtegō, -ere, -texī, -tectum - *to protect, defend against*
prōvincia, -ae, f. - *special function, command*
proximus, -a, -um - *nearest, next*
puella, -ae, f. - *girl*
pudor, -dōris, m. - *shame, modesty*
puer, puerī, m. - *boy;* pl. *boys, children*
pugnō (1) - *to fight*
pulcher, -chra, -chrum - *beautiful, handsome*
pulchritūdō, -dinis, f. - *beauty*
pulvis, -veris, m. - *dust*
pūrgō (1) - *to clean, wash*
putō (1) - *to think, consider*
Pythia, -ae, f. - *Pythia*, the priestess, seer of Apollo at Delphi

Q

quam (adv.) - *how*
quamquam (conj.) - *although*
quandōcumque (adv.) - *whenever, as often as*
quāre (adv.) - *therefore, wherefore, why*
quattuor (indeclinable adj.) - *four*
quārtus, -a, -um - *fourth*
quī, quae, quod (rel. pron.) - *who, which, what, that;* (interrogative adj.) - *what? which? what kind of?*
quīdam, quaedam, quiddam or **quoddam** (indefinite pron. and adj.) - *a certain one, thing; some*
quīntus, -a, -um - *fifth*
quis, quid - *who?, what?*
quisque, quaeque, quidque - *each one, every one*
quisquis, quisquid - *whoever, whatever*
quō (adv.) - *to where?/whither?; where, in which place*
quod (conj.) - *because*
quōmodo (adv.) - *how, in what way*
quoniam (conj.) - *since, inasmuch as*
quoque (adv.) - *also, too*
quotannīs (adv.) - *yearly*
quotiēns (adv.) - *as often as, whenever*
quotiēnscumque (adv.) - *however often, whenever*

R

rāmus, -ī, m. - *bough, branch, twig*
rapiō, -ere, rapuī, raptum - *to seize, snatch, carry away*
ratiō, -tiōnis, f. - *reckoning, account; reason, judgment, consideration; system, manner, method*

recēdō, -ere, -cessī, -cessum - *to go back, retire, recede*
recipiō, -ere, -cēpī, -ceptum - *to gain possession of, get back*
recūsō (1) - *to refuse*
redeō, -īre, -iī, -itum - *to go back, return*
redūcō, -ere, -dūxī, -ductum - *to lead back, bring back*
referō, -ferre, -ttulī, -lātum - *to bring back*
rēgīna, -ae, f. - *queen*
rēgnō (1) - *to rule*
rēgnum, -ī, n. - *kingdom*
regō, -ere, rēxī, rēctum - *to rule, guide, direct*
relinquō, -ere, -līquī, -lictum - *to leave behind, leave, abandon*
reliquus, -a, -um - *remaining, rest*
remaneō, -ēre, -mānsī, -mānsūrus - *to remain, stay behind*
rēmus, -ī, m. - *oar*
remōtus, -a, -um - *remote, distant*
removeō, -ēre, -mōvī, -mōtum - *to remove*
reperiō, -īre, -pperī, -pertum - *to find, discover, learn*
repugnō (1) (+ dat.) - *to fight against*
rēs, reī, f. - *thing, matter, business, affair*
resolvō, -ere, -solvī, -solūtum - *to loosen, untie*
respondeō, -ēre, -spondī, -spōnsum - *to respond, answer, reply*
respōnsum, -ī, n. - *response, answer*
restituō, -ere, -uī, -ūtum - *to replace, restore*
reveniō, -īre, -vēnī, -ventum - *to come back, return*
revocō (1) - *to call back, recall*
rēx, rēgis, m. - *king*
rīdeō, -ēre, rīsī, rīsum - *to laugh, smile*
rītus, -ūs, m. - *rite, ceremony*
rogō (1) - *to ask*
Rōma, -ae, f. - *Rome*
Rōmānī, -ōrum, m. pl. - *the Romans*
Rōmulus, -ī, m. - *Romulus, son of Mars, founder of Rome*
rūmor, -mōris, m. - *rumor, gossip*
ruō, -ere, ruī, rutum - *to rush, fall, be ruined*
rūpēs, -is, f. - *steep, rocky cliff; crag*
rursum (adv.) - *again*

S

saepe (adv.) - *often*
sacer, -cra, -crum - *sacred*
sacerdōs, -dōtis, m. - *priest*
sacrificium, -iī, n. - *sacrifice*
sacrificō (1) - *to perform a sacrifice, offer a sacrifice*
saevus, -a, -um - *harsh, savage, cruel*
sagitta, -ae, f. - *arrow*
salūtō (1) - *to welcome, greet*
salvus, -a, -um - *safe, sound*
sānctus, -a, -um - *holy, sacred*
sapienter (adv.) - *wisely*
Sāturnus, -ī, m. - *Saturn*, a Titan; the Greek Cronus
satyrus, -ī, m. - *satyr*, a demi-god of wild places; half-man, half-goat
saxum, -ī, n. - *rock, stone*
scandō, -ere, scandī, scānsum - *to climb, mount*
scelerātus, -a, -um - *wicked, accursed*
scelus, -leris, n. - *evil deed, crime, sin, wickedness*
scientia, -ae, f. - *knowledge, skill*
sciō, -īre, -īvī, -ītum - *to know*
scrībō, -ere, scrīpsī, scrīptum - *to write, compose*
scrīptor, -tōris, m. - *writer, author*

sē (third person reflexive pronun) - *himself, herself, itself, themselves*
sēcrētum, -ī, n. - *secret*
sed (conj.) - *but*
sedeō, -ēre, sēdī, sessum - *to sit*
sēmen, -minis, n. - *seed, stock, race*
semper (adv.) - *always*
senectūs, -tūtis, f. - *old age*
senex, senis, m. (adj. and noun) - *old, old man*
senior, -ius - *older, elder*
sēnsus, -ūs, m. - *feeling, sense*
sentiō, -īre, sēnsī, sēnsum - *to feel perceive, think, experience*
sēparō (1) - *to separate, divide*
septem - (indeclinable adj.) -*seven*
sērō (adv.) - *too late, late*
serpēns, -pentis, m./f. - *serpent, snake*
servitūs, -tūtis, f. - *servitude, slavery*
servō (1) - *to preserve, keep, save, guard*
servus, -ī, m./serva, -ae, f. - *slave*
sex (indeclinable adj.) - *six*
sī (conj.) - *if*
sīc (adv.) - *so, thus*
signum, -ī, n. - *sign, signal, indication*
silēns, -lentis - *silent*
sileō, -ēre, -uī - *to be silent*
silva, -ae, f. - *forest*
similis, -e (+ dat.) - *like*
simul (adv.) - *at the same time*
sine (prep. + abl.) - *without*
sinister, -tra, -trum - *left, left-hand, harmful, ill-omened*
sōl, sōlis, m. - *sun*
soleō, -ēre, solitus sum - *to be accustomed to*
sōlum (adv.) - *only*
sōlus, -a, -um - *alone, only*
nōn sōlum ... sed etiam: *not only ... but also*

solvō, -ere, soluī, -ūtum - *to loosen, undo, untie*
somnus, -ī, m. - *sleep*
soror, -rōris, f. - *sister*
sors, sortis, f. - *oracular pronouncement, prophecy*
spargō, -ere, spārsī, spārsum - *to scatter, spread, strew*
speciēs, -ēī, f. - *appearance, look*
spectāculum, -ī, n. - *spectacle, sight*
spectātor, -tōris, m. - *spectator, viewer*
spectō (1) - *to look at, see*
spēlunca, -ae, f. - *cave, cavern*
spernō, -ere, sprēvī, sprētum - *to scorn, despise, spurn*
spērō (1) - *to hope for, hope*
spēs, spēī, f. - *hope*
spīritus, -ūs, m. - *breath, breathing, spirit, soul*
sponte: ablative, *will, accord*
statim (adv.) - *immediately*
statuō, -ere, -uī, -ūtum - *to decide*
stō, stāre, stetī, statum - *to stand, stand still or firm*
strangulō (1) - *to strangle, choke, throttle*
studium, -iī, n. - *eagerness, zeal, pursuit, study*
sub (prep. + abl.) - *under*
subitō (adv.) - *suddenly*
suī, sibi, sē, sē (third person reflexive pronoun) - *himself, herself, itself, themselves*
sum, esse, fuī, futūrus (irregular) - *to be*
superbia, -ae, f. - *arrogance, pride*
superbus, -a, -um - *arrogant, overbearing, haughty, proud*
superō (1) - *to overcome, conquer*
supersum, -esse, -fuī, -futūrus - *to remain*
suprēmus, -a, -um - *highest*
suscēnseō, -ēre, -uī - *to be angry*

suscipiō, -ere, -cēpī, -ceptum - *to undertake, take on, assume*

suspendō, -ere, -pendī, -pēnsum - *to hang, hang up, suspend*

sustineō, -ēre, -tenuī, -tentum - *to hold up, sustain*

sustollō, -ere - *to lift up, raise*

suus, -a, -um - *his own, her own, its own; their own*

T

tālis, -e - *such*

tam (adv. used to intensify adjectives and adverbs) - *so*

tamen (adv.) - *nevertheless, still*

tandem (adv.) - *at last, finally*

tangō, -ere, tetigī, tāctum - *to touch*

tantus, -a, -um - *so large, so great*

Tartarus, -ī, m. - *Tartarus*, the underworld

taurus, -ī, m. - *bull*

tē (acc. s. of **tū**) - *you*

tēctum, -ī, n. - *shelter, house*

tegō, -ere, tēxī, tēctum - *to cover, hide, protect*

tēlum, -ī, n. - *spear, weapon*

tempestās, -tātis, f. - *season, weather; storm*

templum, -ī, n. - *temple*

temptō (1) - *to try*

tempus, -poris, n. - *time, season*

teneō, -ēre, -uī, tentum - *to hold, keep, possess*

tenuis, -e - *delicate, fine, slender*

ter (adv.) - *three times, thrice*

tergum, -ī, n. - *back*

terminō (1) - *to end*

terra, -ae, f. - *land, country, earth*

terreō, -ere, -uī, -itum - *to frighten, terrify*

terribilis, -e - *inspiring terror, terrifying*

terror, -rōris, m. - *terror*

tertius, -a, -um - *third*

Thetis, -idis, f. - *Thetis*, a Nereid, a sea-nymph, mother of Achilles

timeō, -ēre, -uī - *to fear, be afraid of*

timidus, -a, -um - *fearful*

timor, -ōris, m. - *fear*

tingō, -ere, tīnxī, tīnctum - *to wet, moisten*

Tīresiās, -ae, m. - *Tiresias*, legendary blind prophet of Thebes

Tītānus, -ī, m. - *Titan* (the second generation of gods)

tolerō (1) - *to bear, endure, tolerate*

tollō, -ere, sustulī, sublātum - *to raise, lift up; take away, destroy*

tonitrus, -ūs, m. - *thunder*

tot (indeclinable adj.) - *so many*

tōtus, -a, -um - *whole, entire*

tragoedia, -ae, f. - *tragedy*

trahō, -ere, trāxī, tractum - *to draw, drag, derive; attract, fascinate*

trāns (prep. + acc.) - *across*

trēs, tria - *three*

trīdēns, -dentis, m. - *trident, three-pronged spear*

trīstis, -e - *sad, sorrowful; grim*

Trōia, -ae, f. - *Troy*, city in western Turkey

Trōiānus, -a, -um - *Trojan*

tū, tuī, tibi, tē, tē - *you* (s.)

tum (adv.) - *then*

tumultus, -ūs, m. - *uprising, disturbance, tumult*

turba, -ae, f. - *crowd, mob; uproar*

tūtus, -a, -um - *safe*

U

ubi (rel. adv. and conj.) - *where;* (interrogative) *when*
Ulixēs, -is, m. - *Ulysses,* the Greek Odysseus, king of Ithaca
ūllus, -a, -um - *any*
ulterius (adv.) - *further*
ultimus, -a, -um - *last, final*
umerus, -ī, m. - *shoulder, upper arm*
ūnā (adv.) - *together*
unda, -ae, f. - *wave*
undique (adv.) - *on all sides, everywhere*
ūnus, -a, -um - *one, single, alone*
Ūranus, -ī, m. - *Uranus,* sky god, son and spouse of Gaia
urbs, urbis, f. - *city*
ut (conj.) with indicative - *as;* with subjunctive - *that, so that*
uter, -tra, -trum - *either, which (of two)*
uxor, uxōris, f. - *wife*

V

vacuus, -a, -um - *empty*
validus, -a, -um - *strong*
vastus, -a, -um - *vast, enormous*
vātēs, -is, m. - *prophet, seer*
vel (conj.) - *or*
vēlō (1) - *to conceal by covering, wrap*
vēlum -ī, n. - *sail*
vēnātrix -trīcis, f. - *huntress*
venia, -ae, f. - *pardon, forgiveness*
veniō, -īre, vēnī, ventum - *to come*
ventus, -ī, m. - *wind*
Venus, -neris, f. - *Venus,* goddess of love, the Greek Aphrodite
vēr, vēris, n. - *spring* (the season)
verbum, -ī, n. - *word*
vēritās, -tātis, f. - *truth*
vertō, -ere, vertī, versum - *to turn, change*
vērus, -a, -um - *true, real*
vesper, -peris, m. - *evening*
Vesta, -ae, f. - *Vesta,* goddess of the hearth
Vestālis, -is, f. - *Vestal virgin,* keeper of the sacred flame of Rome
vestīgium -iī, n. - *footstep, track*
vestis, -is, f. - *clothing*
vexō (1) - *to ravage, afflict*
via, -ae, f. - *way, road*
victōria, -ae, f. - *victory*
videō, vidēre, vīdī, vīsum - *to see*
videor, vidērī, vīsus sum - *to be seen, seem, appear*
vincō, -ere, vīcī, victum - *to conquer, overcome*
vinculum, -ī, n. - *chain*
vīnum, -ī, n. - *wine*
violō (1) - *to violate*
vir, virī, m. - *man*
virgō, -ginis, f. - *maiden, virgin*
vīs, vīs, f. - *force, power, violence*
vīta, -ae, f. - *life*
vitium, -iī, n. - *fault, vice, crime*
vītō (1) - *to avoid, shun*
vīvō, -ere, vīxī, vīctum - *to live*
vīvus, -a, -um - *alive, living*
vocō (1) - *to call*
Volcānus, -ī, m. - *Vulcan,* god of fire, the Greek Hephaistus
volō, velle, voluī - *to wish*
voluptās, -tātis, f. - *pleasure*
vōmer, -meris, m. - *plowshare, plow*
vorō (1) - *to swallow, devour*
voveō, -ēre, vōvī, vōtum - *to vow, promise*
vōx, vōcis, f. *voice, word*
vulnus, -eris, n. - *wound*
vultus, -ūs, m. *face; appearance, look, aspect*

LATIN READERS TO BUILD READING SPEED AND CONFIDENCE

Ease into Reading Livy's History
READING LIVY'S ROME
Selections from Books I–VI of Livy's *Ab Urbe Condita*
Milena Minkova and Terence Tunberg
Student Text: xii + 276 pp., 6 b&w illustrations (2005) 6" x 9" Paperback, ISBN 978-0-86516-550-2
Teacher's Guide: 112 pp. (2005) 6" x 9" Paperback, ISBN 978-0-86516-600-4

Let a Monkey Teach Latin!
THE ADVENTURES OF THE MONKEY PILOSUS NASO
Res Gestae Simii Pilosi Nasonis
Thomas E. Hayes
Student Text: xvii + 219 pp., 49 line drawings + 10 halftones (2005)
6" x 9" Paperback, ISBN 978-0-86516-453-6
Teacher's Guide: 37 pp. (2005) 8½" x 11" Paperback, ISBN 978-0-86516-497-0

The Bridge to Reading Vergil
VERGIL: A LEGAMUS Transitional Reader
Thomas J. Sienkewicz and LeaAnn A. Osburn
xxiv + 136 pp., line drawings (2004) 8½" x 11" Paperback, ISBN 978-0-86516-578-6

The Bridge to Reading Catullus
CATULLUS: A LEGAMUS Transitional Reader
Kenneth F. Kitchell Jr. & Sean Smith
xxx + 160 pp. (2006) 8½" x 11" Paperback, ISBN 978-0-86516-634-9

A Classic Beginning/Intermediate Reader
CIVIS ROMANUS: A Reader for the First Two Years of Latin
Cobban & Colebourn
xii + 128 pp. (2003 reprint of 1967 edition) 6" x 9" Paperback, ISBN 978-0-86516-569-4

A Best-selling Reader for the First Year
38 LATIN STORIES
Anne H. Groton and James M. May
Student Text: vi + 104 pp. (1995, 5th edition) 6" x 9" Paperback, ISBN 978-0-86516-289-1
Teacher's Guide: 23 pp. (2004) 6" x 9" Paperback, ISBN 978-0-86516-591-5

Graded Readings on Legendary Latin History
ROME AND HER KINGS
Livy I: Graded Selections
W. D. Lowe and C. E. Freeman
110 pp., Maps (1988, reprint 2000) 6" x 9" Paperback, ISBN 978-0-86516-450-5

Engaging Neo-Latin Reader in Classical Latin Style
COLUMBUS' FIRST VOYAGE
Latin Selections from Peter Martyr's *De Orbe Novo*
Constance P. Iacona and Edward V. George
xvi + 40 pp., 5 b&w reproduction images (2005) 6" x 9" Paperback, ISBN 978-0-86516-613-4

BOLCHAZY-CARDUCCI PUBLISHERS, INC.
WWW.BOLCHAZY.COM